From Dora, M. Kinnear. Wit
to Derek on this your special Birthday -
1998.

St Mary's Church, Witney

Mill, Burford

Burford

Worsham Mill.

Minster Lovell Ruins

Swinbrook
Widford
Minster Lovell
Ruins
Crawley
pton
Asthall
Mill
Witney
Cogges
Cokethorpe
Park
Ducklington
Fritillaries at
Ducklington
Hardwick
Beard Mill
Standlake
Newbridge

Widford Church
and deserted village

WHERE THE WINDRUSH FLOWS

and will forever flow

WHERE THE WINDRUSH FLOWS

and will forever flow

MOLLIE HARRIS

Illustrations GARY WOODLEY

ALAN SUTTON

First published in the United Kingdom in 1989
Alan Sutton Publishing Limited, Brunswick Road, Gloucester

First published in the United States of America in 1990
Alan Sutton Publishing Inc., Wolfeboro Falls, NH 03896–0848

British Library Cataloguing in Publication Data

Harris, Mollie
Where the Windrush Flows.
1. England. Cotswolds
I. Title
942.4′170858

ISBN 0-86299-680-5

Library of Congress Cataloging in Publication Data
applied for

Designed by Martin Latham

Typesetting and origination by
Alan Sutton Publishing Limited.
Colour separation by
J. Films Process Co. Limited.
Printed in Italy by New Interlitho S.p.A.

To all the folk on Windrush side
who helped to make this book possible.

Mollie Harris

Contents

Foreword

BY NORMAN PAINTING

(Phil Archer in the BBC's long running programme *The Archers*)

This is the story of a journey, a quest; and for most of us such stories are irresistible, as they have been from the very earliest times. It is a true story, too: one has only to read a few lines to be reassured that this is no fanciful country book, concocted in some city library, but a labour of love written on the spot. Every phrase breathless authenticity, whether it describes flora and fauna, people past and present, customs, sayings of folklore; or whether the author is sharing her own reflections on what she actually sees, in her highly personal and idiosyncratic language. And because she is not pretending to be anything other than she is – a pleasant, observant, sociable and highly intelligent country woman – she is never in the least inhibited about using dialect words and phrases and local names for plants and pastimes. You will find splendid descriptive words like loppeting, swabble, chacketing, dimpsey, clombering and fithering, names for country games, like iddy-iddy onker, which in my Warwickshire childhood we called by the simpler name of conkers; and country children's names for plants and fruits, such as Snotty-gozzles, Granny's nightcaps and Shimmy-shirts.

Mollie Harris leads her readers on a personally conducted tour of the course of the river Windrush, from its source in the Cotswolds to where it merges with the Thames in Oxfordshire. I was particularly pleased to be asked by my old friend and colleague to write this Foreword, as the journey it tells of passes through the land of some of my forebears as well as of hers. Only a few years ago – having steadily insisted from the time I took part in the very first episode of the radio programme *The Archers* that I came from a family of coal-mining and railway workers – did I learn that before settling in Hook Norton in Oxfordshire, my great grandfather was a shepherd near Burford: and Burford has a whole chapter to itself in this delightful book.

Having been born on St George's Day, 23 April, I was fascinated to learn that on that day one should gather dandelions to make wine – but only if the sun is shining!

There is much in this book, perhaps inevitably in the story of a river, about watermills – whether for fulling, or for grinding corn and cattle feed. And besides sharing her enthusiasm for the trees, shrubs and wild flowers of the region, the author is equally enthusiastic about the people, the villages (well, most of them!), and the stone quarries from which nearly all the buildings along the river Windrush are built. As an Oxford man I noted with interest that, according to Mollie Harris, much of the stone for my own College, Christ Church, came from quarries near the Windrush.

So, let Mollie Harris be your guide as she traces the course of the Windrush. Through her eyes, see familiar things afresh; pollard willows 'like giant shaving brushes', or pussy-willows 'looking like day-old chicks'. Travel hopefully with her through Cotswold villages, through history from Roman times to the present day, with always an amusing or informative comment on all she sees and everyone she encounters until, its own journey ended, the river Windrush disappears into Mother Thames and continues onward to the open sea.

Reed Bunting

The many readers of Mollie Harris's previous books will, of course, know what delights are in store: those unfamiliar with her work may well be encouraged to start with this one – for she has done nothing better. It is a book to savour and cherish, for on every page you can breathe country air in the company of an expert guide and a most engaging companion.

Acknowledgements

I would like to thank everyone who kindly told me little stories and anecdotes on my journey along the Windrush, especially Mrs Barton, Mike Cavanagh, Dr Clegg, Mrs A. Coles, Ann Cooper, Sally Craig, Tony and Charlie Dale, Richard Early, Mrs Finlason, Elinor Garner, Guiting Power W.I., Bill, Brian and David Hall, Patricia Hamilton, Mr Harris, Mr and Mrs Hudson, and Mrs Hudson senior, George Laughton, John Matthews, Mr N. Mills, Mrs Peel, Anne Perrin, Judy and Paul Rose, Mr and Mrs H. Taylor, Mrs Joan Taylor, Jack Turner, Harry Trinder, Mrs Walker and Mr Wiltshire, Mrs Wise, and the landlady of The Plough.

My main sources of information for this exploration were Edith Brill's *Life and Traditions on the Cotswolds* (Dent, 1973; Alan Sutton Publishing, 1987) and *Companion into Oxfordshire* by Ethel Carleton Williams (Methuen, 1935) – as well as several booklets from the churches I visited along the way.

Song of the Windrush

A little stream sets out with pride
To brave the Cotswold countryside.
Temple Guiting, calmer still,
Then the race at Harford Mill.
Once in Bourton's spacious green
(Venice of the Cotswold scene)
Lingering under bridges grey
Nursed by trees it longed to stay.
Now, when Mammon's noisy greed
Crowds its banks, it gathers speed.
Sherborne, Windrush, Taynton gleam
Jewels on the Windrush stream
Burford's hill serene and grey
Holds the ghost of Cromwell's day.
On to Swinbrook's lovely peace
Church and bridge and water leas.
Where the Fettiplaces lie
In their marble dignity.
Now it glides by Minster Hall
Dreaming of the Lovells' fall.
Till in Witney's busy maze
Lost, it broods on other days.
Comforted to serve the mill
Where its wool is treasure still.
Then with wearying twist and bend
Standlake fields bring journey's end
Newbridge arch, its travel done
Mother Thames receives her son.

by Charles L. Harris
(no relation)

Introduction

This is the story of the river Windrush, a quiet, winding river meandering through valleys flanked by Cotswold hills and lush meadows for most of its thirty mile journey before it joins up with the Thames at Newbridge in Oxfordshire.

Apparently the old name for Windrush was 'Wenrisc', derived at some time from two separate words – *wen*, which in Anglo-Saxon means wind, and *risc* meaning rush or reed. Over the years it has become one word, 'Windrush', which describes its character exactly: it winds through the rushes. And wind it certainly does, too, twisting and turning through much of Gloucestershire and part of Oxfordshire. In some places it is much more winding than in others, with no fewer than eight double S-bends in a matter of a quarter of a mile.

Today there are at least seventeen villages and three towns which straddle the Windrush, and there is evidence of settlements on those spots since man first made his home there because of the water – for water is the necessity of life. Stone Age, Iron Age, Romans and Saxons, all settled along its banks. Here, through the centuries, men built cottages and mansions, farms and homesteads, shaping the villages with the stone that was already under their feet. There too were the special stones which, when split by frost, provided slates for roofing. Many mills, flour and fulling mills, cloth and blanket mills, were built along that thirty mile stretch; most villages had one, some had two or more, and in their day they provided work for the local people, as well as flour to see them through the cold winters and cloth and blankets to warm their very bones. And it was the Windrush that provided the power which sent the mill-wheels clicking, clacking and turning.

Stone quarries were opened in most parishes, providing material not only for the villagers, but for use much further afield. Until the coming of rail and motor transport, stone was taken by road in huge wagons pulled by several horses to a point at Radcot on the Thames; from there on it went by barge to London to help build St Paul's Cathedral, and many other prominent buildings. Colleges and churches, barns and monasteries, were built from stone from these quarries. Some of them remain open today, for there is a great demand for 'dressed stone', either for building new houses and mansions or repairing old ones. Stone is also needed for renewing the Cotswold stone walls that run for miles through parts of the Windrush Valley.

And so this river, which starts its life as a shy trickle in a pasture high above the village of Cutsdean, ambles on along its journey, starting like a baby – small and gentle – then gradually growing and gaining strength through places like Ford, Temple Guiting, Kineton and Naunton. Not until it reaches Bourton-on-the-Water does it suddenly become a grown-up river, bringing both beauty and prosperity to the town. Then, having done a good job there, it goes on to meander through low-lying green meadows, always winding, twisting and turning, through the delightful villages of Windrush, Great and Little Barrington and Taynton, until it reaches Burford with its lovely stone bridge at the bottom of the famous High Street. Then it is off again, gently gliding through the pretty villages of Widford, Swinbrook, Asthall, Minster Lovell and Crawley, until it reaches Witney, where – to use Henry Taunt's words – 'It whitens Witney blankets'; without the properties of the river there would not have been the world-famous Witney blanket mills. From then on, the Windrush leaves the Cotswolds behind and wanders dreamily through the flat flower-filled fields of Oxfordshire, winding its way through the fritillary meadows of Ducklington, then on to the villages of Hardwick and Standlake until it comes to the end of its journey, gliding under the old stone bridge at Newbridge to vanish out of sight as it flows unobtrusively into the Thames.

It was on a lovely blue and white August day that I journeyed to the village of Cutsdean and then on to Taddington where, I was told, the source of the river Windrush rises. 'Look out for Field Barn, which lies two or three fields from the road – it's somewhere near there.' On each side of the narrow road the verges were massed with late summer flowers – brilliant blue meadow cranesbill, tall rosebay willowherb, creamy meadowsweet and purple knapweed. Giant hog or pigweed, tall as a man, stood

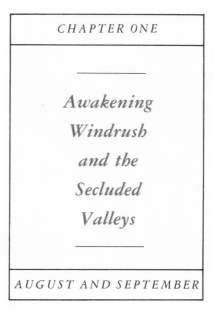

like sentinels everywhere, and the rolling Cotswold hills were all around.

Typical Cotswold dry stone wall

I turned off down a lane, high-banked with hawthorn bushes, with parts of a disused wall showing here and there, and climbing all over the bushes were masses of giant convolvulus; as children we used to pick these white flowers, turn them upside down and push the stem of a stiff grass into the centre of the flower – and that we called a doll's parasol or a fairy parasol: other country names for the flowers are Granny's nightcap

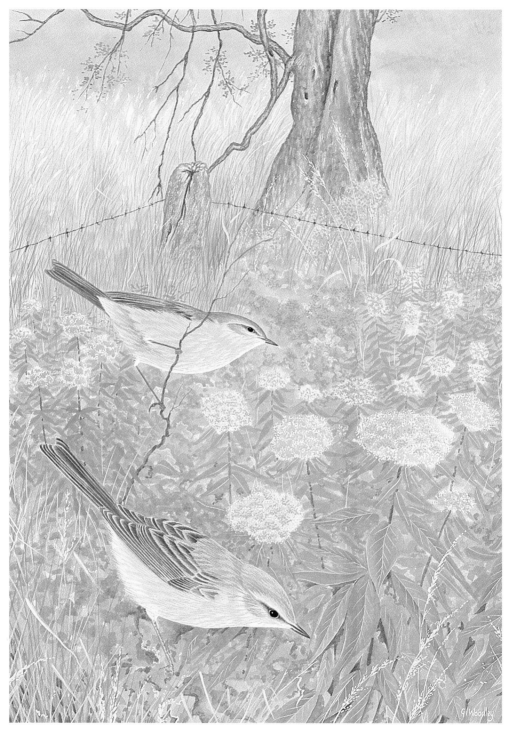

Willow warblers flitted and chirruped in front of me

————————

and Shimmy shirts. Pollen from a multitude of grasses puffed off as I brushed by. I could see the buildings of Field Barn (now made into a lovely house) in front of me, and away to my right a very large plot of uncultivated ground massed with water-loving weeds and reeds. I strolled over, but there was no water! I followed a narrow line of reeds and rushes for a little way, and came to a small stone bridge, which I understand is called 'Dirty Brook Bridge'. Here a narrow deep ditch, which was fenced off, ran alongside a meadow. I clambered over the bridge and walked by the side of the ditch; still there was no water, but I would think that in winter there would be. A family of willow warblers flitted and chirruped just in front of me as I walked along the side of the fence; huge clumps of codlins-and-cream, a tall plant with lots of creamy pink flowers on the top, were growing in the ditch.

Then, suddenly – because several swallows were flying low and dipping into a little hollow just to my right – I stopped and looked, and there it was! The birthplace of the Windrush – a very small, crystal clear spring, quietly trickling from the hillside, and forming a little pool not much bigger than a meat dish. There was a flat stone across it and water-mint and forget-me-nots grew around it. I cupped my hand and drank a draught from that life-giving spring. Other little trickles of water from the hillside joined this larger one, making it a 'tiny finger of a river', as someone has described these first few yards of the Windrush.

I gazed ahead, to where my pathway led; the hills and valleys seemed to fold gently into one another. Some of the harvest fields were already cleared of corn; giant, round, golden straw bales now filled those same fields and here and there some early ploughing had been done, the rich red-brown earth furrowed and tidy ready for the autumn planting. A mile or so along that low-lying valley I came to Cutsdean, the first village on the banks of the river Windrush. Here, several little springs seemed to bubble and trickle from nowhere, to fall into the river – even so, it was still only about two yards wide at this point, and still banked on either side with wild flowers, rushes and reed mace.

One spring ran alongside a cottage, whose garden was a joy to see. There were masses of flowers in front of the cottage, brilliant orange lilies, phlox, stocks and roses, and then row upon row of vegetables – onions, peas, broad beans, potatoes, beetroot, parsnip and a row of stick runner beans – enough for now and for all the winter was planted there; truly a countryman's garden, I thought.

A tiny spring trickling from the hillside

I stood gazing admiringly at the well-kept plot.

A man came out of the cottage and said 'good morning'.

'My word,' I remarked, 'a lot of hard work has gone into your garden to make it look like this.'

'Ah, yes,' he replied, 'but being country born and bred a garden like this comes natural. It goes back to the days when wages was very small, and you had to grow most of your own grub to survive.'

'Been here long?' I asked.

'My parents brought me to this cottage when I was four months old, and I've been here ever since, and I'm turned seventy now.'

Turned seventy, and not a weed to be seen in that lovely garden!

I walked up the hill to have a look round the village. It was very small, just a huddle of Cotswold stone cottages and a couple of farms, with no pub or school, but a beautiful little well-kept church which you can reach from Cutsdean farmyard. In the church porch I read about the history of the church, and also an apology from the vicar: 'The altar looks bare because someone stole our candlesticks on September 7th, 1978'.

Cutsdean Farm is a collection of lovely Cotswold buildings with a long open cart-shed supported by huge pillars on staddle-stones; there are several lofty barns and out-buildings, the sort that if they could speak would be able to recall the prosperous days of the wool trade which brought wealth and fame to the Cotswolds. Now all was quiet in the farmyard, no pigs, no cattle, just bales of straw in the barns, and modern farm machinery in the yards.

I strolled back down the village street, where the old gardener was still busy working on his plot.

'How far is it to Ford along the fields?' I asked.

'Oh, 'tis only about half a mile. You see,' he went on, 'before folks had bikes and cars that was a short cut to Ford, quicker than going round the roadway, and more pleasant, of course, in summer-time, too,' he said.

More pleasant, indeed. All around were the rolling hills that are Cotswold, and

Truly a countryman's garden

———

here and there flocks of sheep grazed contentedly.

At Ford the river was only about two to three yards wide and still banked on either side with wild flowers.

Ford is just a collection of cottages with a couple of larger houses. There was a farm, but now quite a few of the farm buildings have been made into houses. But the inn there – The Plough – is quite a famous hostelry; a rambling building, and one of the oldest inns in England. It was once a courthouse where men were tried and hanged for sheep stealing. The cellar there was used as a jail, and built into one of the bar walls are the remains of the stocks into which the prisoners were locked. The lady at the inn told me 'Ah, they used to try 'um in here, and then take 'um up there' – nodding towards the hill which rose high above the hamlet – 'and hang 'um on a gibbet.'

Before I left Ford, I stopped to read the plaque set in the wall of The Plough Inn:

Ye weary travellers that pass by.
With dust and scorching sunbeams dry
Or be be-numb'd with snow and frost.
With having these bleak cotswolds crosst.
Step in and quaff my nut brown ale
Bright as rubys mild and stale.
Twill make your laging trotters dance
As nimble as the suns of France.
Then ye will own ye men of sense
That neare was better spent six pence.

Legend claims that William Shakespeare wrote it in lieu of a night's lodging.

I took the high road to Temple Guiting, the next village on the Windrush. From the roadway I sometimes caught a glimpse of the river as it wound along.

7

Here the hills seem to be pitched deep into the valley, forming small gorges, with patches of woodland and scrub on the hillsides where a few rooks flapped and chattered.

As I reached Temple Guiting I noticed a little lane-cum-path leading down towards the river, so I wandered down as far as I could. Still there was much growth of reeds and flowers leaning in towards the river, making it look even more narrow than it really was, but I wouldn't think that it was still any more than three yards wide at this point. To the right, and up-river, I could see a large expanse of water and a bridge. 'Surely,' I thought, 'the Windrush hasn't suddenly got that wide!' Later, I was to learn why.

Temple Guiting takes its name from the Knights Templar, who built up a community there. The village is full of delightful Cotswold stone buildings, not two cottages alike, but so warm and simple in such a lovely setting. High on a bank and near the bridge is the Manor House, with mullioned windows and beautiful stone-carved doorways. I noticed that some builders were busy working on the house, so I called and asked if I could look at the famous Dove or Pigeon Cote there. A pretty young woman came to my aid. She and her husband and a lovely baby are the present owners. She told me, 'There's not one dovecote, but two, actually, built on to the house, which is very unusual. You're welcome to look round,' she said. 'Excuse me, I can hear my son crying.'

While she went off indoors to give him his dinner, I walked round the outside towards the dovecotes. One entrance – the first and the biggest – is at the back of the house, and the second is on the west side, looking out on to the garden. It is only the two cupolas on the roof, where the birds entered and left, that proved from the outside what that part of the building was used for. I opened the low-pitched door, which was only about four feet high (was that because people were smaller in those far-off days?), and peeped in. Hundreds and hundreds of nest holes were built all around and into the high walls, which were two to three feet thick. There was enough room for 2500 birds in those two dovecotes: these would have provided the folk living there with plenty of fresh meat and eggs during the winter.

Later, over a cup of coffee, the owner told me that the Manor was first built in 1380 in the reign of Richard II, with many additions and alterations made in Tudor times, and later. In fact, the dovecote was not built until 1747. During the reign of Henry VIII, Bishop Fox lived in the Manor. He was a very influential person, and was highly thought of by Henry. During the time he was living at Temple Guiting he became Chaplain to Katherine of Aragon. He also founded Corpus Christi College in Oxford, became a benefactor of Magdalen College, Oxford, and Pembroke at Cambridge, and did much for education generally during his lifetime. At some time, it is said, the Manor became the summer palace of the Bishops of Worcester and Oxford.

Over the roadbridge I could see yet another lovely, big, important-looking Cotswold building. A council worker told me that it was Temple Guiting House. He also said that he had always understood that the sudden expanse of water I had seen was where the river had been dug out years ago to provide a lake and fishing facilities for a one-time owner of the Manor.

Thankfully I noticed, as I made my way out of Temple Guiting and towards Kineton, that my river had become its normal width again. The valley was tree-filled and shady, and the Windrush flowed lazily along past fields dotted with sheep and cattle standing motionless under the shade of the trees.

Kineton is another very lovely old

Cotswold village, with a delightful inn called the Halfway House, where both the landlord and his friendly boxer dog, Albert, made me most welcome. I asked about the 'clapper' bridge that I understood was built over the Windrush.

'Just take a walk towards the river, and you'll come to it.'

Outside in the sunshine I took first one and then another little lane towards the river, sometimes to find that I was in someone's back garden. Then I found a much longer lane,

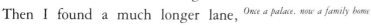

Once a palace, now a family home

where the verges were overgrown with the tallest stinging nettles I'd ever seen; they smelt very strong, too – and not altogether pleasant. At the end of it I found, not a clapper bridge, but a small wooden foot-bridge and a ford, where in the old days farm horses and carts piled high with harvest would have splashed their way through from meadow to farm. I paddled in the shallow ford, a few warblers flew up in front of me, gnats and flies hovered over the water, and the overhanging trees gave a welcome shade. I wandered down the lane for a while, keeping to the water's edge where a few late forget-me-nots bloomed and still plenty of rosebay willowherb and meadowsweet flanked the path. A group

Moon daisies

of youngsters were playing Tarzan on a long, thick, rope slung up in a tall tree. I asked them about a clapper bridge, and although I think they were local, not one could come up with the answer. I wended my way back along that tree-lined lane, a little despondent, and decided to make my way to Barton, a small hamlet about a mile way. Round a bend or two and over a small bridge,

Here grew spearmint and forget-me-nots

Kingfisher, waiting for a catch

under which the Windrush flowed, and before I knew it I was through Barton.

Then, coming towards me along the road was a horse and rider. I stopped the car and enquired about the Kineton clapper bridge. The lady rider was delighted to tell me exactly where it was (apparently, down the only little lane that I *hadn't* tried). Then she said, 'I have a super little bridge over the Windrush on my property in Barton. Would you like to come to the farm and take a photo of it before you go back to Kineton?' Then she added, laughing and looking me straight in the eye, 'I also have a two-seater privy that you might be interested in!'

Whether she recognised me from photos in the privy book, or had seen me on television talking about them, I didn't know, but I readily accepted her offer.

The farm and house were a gem, and had me breaking the Tenth Commandment ('Thou shall not covet thy neighbour's house'). I headed down through the orchard to the riverside and to the charming little bridge spanning about a four-yard wide Windrush, with water as clear as crystal as it ran over the stones on the river bed. Here grew spearmint and forget-me-nots. Apparently at Barton, there was – centuries ago – the first fulling mill in England, powered by the Windrush. Now only coots, moorhen and an occasional kingfisher find haven there. The owner said an elderly man who works for her had told her that when he was a young man, he and the other local fellows used to set kingfisher nets to catch the birds – there were so many about then –

and they used to take trout from the river: fish, of course, that the villagers were glad of to help feed their big families.

The two-seater privy, roofless at the time but being carefully restored, was a nice little find.

I drove back to Kineton and down the correct lane – and there it was, a really lovely old stone clapper bridge. The Windrush looked perfect running under it, tree-shaded, lush with late summer

Centuries old stone clapper bridge

greenery, the water dappled blue from the sky overhead. As usual I paddled (I always paddle whenever I can), letting the cool shallow water swirl around my ankles. The water was so clear that you could have read a newspaper, had it been placed on the river bed. A solitary wagtail, perched on a twig near me, protested loudly, as if to claim this Eden as his – and who could blame him.

Cock pheasant, jewel of the fields

The rolling hills and valleys that make up Cotswold country cannot be paralleled anywhere else in England; they seem to possess a wonderful individual beauty, and this is what helps to give the early part of the Windrush valley so much charm. Then there are the miles and miles of dry stone walls which divide the fields and farms, giving a wide vista of an almost patchwork look, with the red soil of a newly ploughed field, green cattle-filled pastures, and fields planted with autumn wheat, the pale green sheen of the corn blades showing.

CHAPTER TWO

"Tis a laughing
little river
where it runs
between the hills'

HENRY TAUNT

OCTOBER

At this time of the year, bright cock pheasants strut about the fields; the hen birds are so dull-looking that it is difficult to see them on ploughed land – very good camouflage, of course. But the male birds with all their wonderful colours remind me of Indian princes, their necks hung with brilliant colourful jewels.

All this I observed as I made my way to Guiting Power, my next port of call along the valley of the Windrush, though the river does not run through the village, but skirts it about half a mile away. This lovely, quiet, Cotswold village lies in a fold of the hills, sort of protected from the winter's blasts. It is not a showplace like Bourton-on-the-Water, but very beautiful, and in 1972 the villagers agreed that it be designated as a Conservation Area within the 'Area of Outstanding Natural Beauty'.

The word 'Guiting' is derived from an Anglo-Saxon word *Gyte*, meaning a pouring out, a torrent. This may have been a good description of the Windrush in this area at the time, but it is very different now, of course, because the river just ripples along – and its ripples, especially around sharp bends, make a sound like the gurgle of babies' laughter. Henry Taunt, the Victorian photographer and writer from Oxford, said of the river: ''Tis a laughing little river where it runs between the hills', and always called it 'The Laughing Windrush'.

There have been folk living here since the Bronze and Iron Ages, and Roman and Saxon finds have been made in the area.

A wonderful little booklet by members of Guiting Power W.I., which I bought at the Post Office, gives a picture of how the village has progressed through the ages, and I think it is worth quoting the part dealing with life during the twentieth century.

In 1934 nineteen cottages in Guiting Power as well as a public house and a smallholding were put on the market. This was a critical event in the life of such a small village community. Some houses were bought by local families, and twelve were bought on a mortgage by a far-sighted young woman, Moya Davidson, who had come to live in the village. She saw the danger that young married couples would be unable to find houses in their own village if there were no cottages to rent. Eleven years later, Mr Frank Washbourn bought these cottages from her to add to the Guiting Power Manor estate.

In 1958 when Mr E.R. Cochrane bought the Manor Estate, it consisted of about a thousand acres and fifty of the hundred houses in the village. Most of these houses were placed in the Guiting Manor Trust, a charity created for the purpose of restoring and modernising the houses for letting. The work was heavily subsidised at first, but the Trust has been self-supporting since 1966. In 1977 the Guiting Manor Amenity Trust replaced the former one, and is designed to secure the future of the village lands and houses and of the

local community. As a charity it pays no Income Tax or Inheritance Tax. Four more houses were bought as they became available and eight flatlets for elderly tenants have been built in converted farm buildings.

The village houses help to give continuity to life in Guiting Power, but it is the people who make its history. Not many Cotswold villages with a population of about three hundred can boast eleven families with three generations living in the village and a primary school with over thirty children. The Trust's policy of choosing its tenants from local families and from people working in or near the village, and also giving priority to young married couples, has given the population balance and stability and has, happily, renewed the trend initiated so courageously in the 1930s by Moya Davidson.

The present village hall was built in 1961. Mr E.R. Cochrane gave the site and money for building and equipment, and grants were received from the Ministry of Education and the Gloucestershire County Council. The villagers raised the balance for equipment. The hall is managed by a village committee and provides a professionally equipped stage, a committee room, kitchen, tea room (opening out on to the playing fields), changing rooms with showers, cloakrooms and a car park. Clubs and societies flourish according to demand, and normally include Football, Cricket, Badminton, Cheery Club, Brownies, Pre-School Playgroup, weekly Day Centre, Gardening Club with annual flower show, and an Art Class and W.I.

And, thankfully, Guiting Power still has its own grocer, baker and Post Office. Quite a few men are employed in the stone quarries nearby and on the local farms, and there is seasonal work at The Rare Animal Breeds Farm Park nearby.

There used to be wonderful country mansion

called Guiting Grange, which stood about half a mile from the village, its huge park surrounded by a lovely stone wall built in the eighteenth century to keep the deer in. The park with its miles of walls still remains, but the 'Big House', which of course at one time provided much work for the villagers, was pulled down in 1970.

Like many other villages along the Windrush valley, Guiting Power had two mills, and was connected with the wool trade and the keeping of Cotswold sheep. Just opposite what was Guiting Grange's main park gate there is a group of houses called 'Dyers' where, it is said, woollen cloth for the cardinals' red robes was dyed.

I came away from the village absolutely enchanted by its wonderful, friendly, atmosphere. It is a very much alive village and community, growing gracefully towards the twenty-first century.

Time to make my way towards Naunton, the next village on the river, so I dropped down once more to the twisting valley of the Windrush. Here along the riverside there was an autumnal smell of damp earth and rotting leaves. The first few early frosts had coloured the hawthorn leaves, so that they were now a delightful mixture of orange, yellow, dark red and green. Here and there the blackberry bushes were smothered with late fruits. I picked a few and ate them (great thirst-quenchers, blackberries are) – soon it will be too late to do this because you shouldn't pick them after 12 October: legend has it that on that particular day the Devil tried to get into heaven, and St Peter, who was guarding the pearly gates, of course wouldn't let him in, but gave him a quick shove, and Old Nick plummeted down to earth and landed in a huge blackberry bush. He was so annoyed that, it is said, he spat furiously on the bush, spoiling the fruit and sending it mouldy. But we in the Cotswolds have another theory: we reckon that he piddled on the bush.

I made my way up on to the Andoversford–Stow Road, and looked down on to Naunton. From there the church and the groups of cottages looked quite small and remote. Then I went round a bend or two and down the hill, where each view of the countryside was beautifully different, until I finally reached the village. It proved to be a much bigger place than I first thought. I looked in the church, reputed to be the only one in the Cotswolds to have a stone pulpit, complete with small canopies and carvings, no doubt made by one of the stone-masons who formerly lived thereabouts. Naunton was once an important

Starlings reap a hedgerow harvest

place for the quarrying of stone slates for roofing, and many of the Oxford Colleges are roofed with slates which came from here. At the bottom of the village, a lovely stone bridge spanned the Windrush, which was now about three yards wide. On the right-hand side there were tidy lawns which swept down to the water's edge: these were the grounds of the Gloucester Council Offices, a group of beautiful Cotswold stone buildings. On the other side of the road, right close to the water's edge, was a delightful cottage; here the Windrush presented a more natural look, its bank reed and rush-filled.

An elderly lady was just coming out of the garden gate. We both smiled and said 'Hello'.

After a while I explained to her that I was writing a book about the river and the villages that lay alongside it, and asked whether she could shed any light on some of Naunton's history.

'Well,' she said, 'I've got something quite historic here; come and have a look.'

She led the way past her front door and along the garden path.

'There, what do you think of that?'

It was an old cider mill and press. It stood under an open stone building supported by great square stone pillars, one doorway at the back leading directly to the river (I had seen this doorway from the bridge when I'd looked over). The main trough of the cider mill, which must have been at least thirty feet in circumference, was made from three great pieces of stone which Mrs Garner told me she understood had come from the Forest of Dean. The centre stone again was massive with a great oak beam going through it. A horse or pony would have been harnessed to this, and the animal would walk round and round, pulling the middle stone as it crushed the apples or pears. The fruit pulp would then have been transferred to the big press which stood in the corner of the building, still with the coarse sacking in where the juices ran through. There was a big stone trough at the bottom of the press for the cider to run into. From there it was syphoned into barrels and casks.

'How long since it's been used?' I asked.

'Oh, 1939,' Mrs Garner replied. 'War stopped all that – until then farmers used to come from miles around so that my father, George Reynolds, could make their fruit into cider and perry.'

'How old is the cider press?' I enquired.

'Well, nobody seems to know. If you ask the old folk they just say that it's been here for as long as they can remember. I suppose it could be a couple of hundred years old.'

'Of course,' she went on, 'years ago there was always plenty of trout and other fish in the Windrush. You could stand at the opening in the cider mill building, or fish from my window in the cottage. I've often heard my father say, "Well, mother, I'll just go and catch a trout or two for our tea." Back he'd come in no time, with four or five good-sized ones. Just rolled in seasoned flour and fried in butter – lovely, they were. But there don't seem to be many fish in there these days, just now and then you can see a couple, but nothing like it used to be.'

Then Mrs Garner showed me the way across the meadow where, she said, there was a lovely old dovecote. I took the field path. In the grass there were tiny harebells still blooming, along with sheep's-bit scabious, clover, knapweed and toadflax, while a herd of young bullocks grazed contentedly on the hillside. I even found a few late mushrooms, white and fresh in the grass. Elderberries and sloes hung ripe in the hedgerows, reminding me to pick some soon for making into wine.

I strolled over to the water's edge and found part of an old sluice gate, the only remains of where at one time a mill stood. The banks of the river were massed with bright yellow monkey-musk flowers and water mint. I picked a few

---

The old cider press

---

leaves and crushed them in my hand – the smell was much stronger than my garden mint at home. There had been rain overnight and the Windrush was quite cloudy. I read somewhere that this is to do with the clay on the river bed – the rain disturbs this, making the water sort of milky-looking. And then there, in front of me, was what I was looking for – a fifteenth-century dovecote, very different from the one at Temple Guiting.

Dove or pigeon cotes must have been a very important part of village life centuries ago; there are not many places along the Windrush which haven't had – and in some cases still have – at least one.

This dovecote, erected in 1460, was in the middle of what must lately have been a farmyard, now high with nettles and old farm machinery. The dovecote stands on its own, and is quite a tall building with four gables with a small window in each, and a cupola on top of the steeply-pitched roof. A ridge of moulding all around the building was put on to keep the rats from climbing into the nest holes, of which there are 1176. I peeped in, and there were several pigeons and doves in there. On the huge beams which span the building were centuries of bird droppings – piles of the stuff, and still being added to! This fifteenth-century dovecote is all that remains of a great manor house which once stood there. Across the river at this point is a delightful little foot-bridge which looks as if somebody from the village had made it a long time ago – the lichen-covered stones look as ancient as the dovecote itself.

At the end of the village there was a mill, now made into a lovely home. All along the banks, from the source to its journey's end, there are signs of how the Windrush was once harnessed to provide power for the little mills.

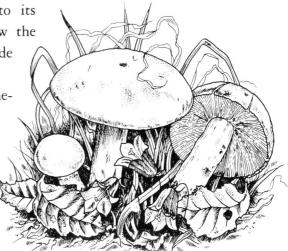

From here on to Bourton-on-the-Water the river widened, but was still rush-bordered. At one place watercress grew in great abundance – perhaps years ago someone gathered it to earn their living. In the old days, before watercress was grown in properly controlled beds, there were

Dovecote at Naunton

only certain months in the year that we countryfolk ate it – when there was an 'R' in the month. It was fine during January, February, March, and April, but after that the streams would most likely be full of frogspawn and other breeding water creatures, so not until September, October, November and December – when the weather became cooler and breeding had stopped – would we go out and gather it again.

At Harford Bridge the Windrush flows under the Cheltenham road, then on and on to remote farmlands and Harford Mill and wood. The beech trees and horse-chestnut were in their full autumn colours and simply dripped with gold. And even here, which seemed miles from anywhere, little boys had been busy;

Iddy-Iddy-Onker

there was evidence of much stick-throwing up into the branches of the horse-chestnut trees, to fetch the conkers down. Big pieces of wood, and leaves, lay thick on the ground. Even so, there were quite a few big fat mahogany-coloured conkers lying about. I picked some up and stuffed them in my pocket: an elderly friend of mine always asks me to get her some each autumn. She calls them 'poor man's mothballs' – and that's what she uses them for, to keep the

Herons loppeting over Lansdowne Bridge

moths away from blankets and other woollens. Anyhow, she says, 'At least they are free, and they don't leave the awful smell that boughten mothballs do.'

As children, we girls made conker furniture from them. For this you needed biggish flat ones. First, we stuck pins around in a semicircle, and then wove wool in and out of the pins, to make a chair-back. Then we fixed four spent matches on the underneath for legs and made super dolls' chairs that way, while our brothers dipped theirs in vinegar and then baked them hard in the fire oven, in an effort to beat the other village lads at Iddy-Iddy-Onker.

There was a lot of ploughing going on, with flocks of gulls and rooks following as the rich red soil was turned over, the birds knowing instinctively that there was lots of food to be found there.

After a while I came again to the Cheltenham road, part of the Old Fosse Way; in fact, at this point there was a Roman-British settlement, where Roman coins and pottery have been found; here, too, rail, river and road once met. But trains no longer run along the now grassy track.

The road, as always, was busy with traffic. I leaned over the stone bridge, sometimes called Lansdowne Bridge – others say that it's the first Bourton Bridge – with the Windrush still gliding underneath. Two herons rose up from the water's edge and flew low, clumsily, loppeting over the field, and in the sky above a huge flock of peewits wheeled and circled. They, like many other birds, go about in great flocks once the breeding season is over and their offspring have flown away.

I took the rough, riverside path into Bourton-on-the-Water, ignoring the lightly built-up area of Lansdowne. Here I saw moorhens and coots, and the willow trees overhung the river. I made my way across a field and down a narrow path, and as I came to the back end of Bourton I could hear the sound

of water, sort of quietly tumbling; here was the back of what was once the last working flour mill in Bourton. It was Windrush water dripping through the old mill's sluice gate that I had heard. I turned left and came out in front of what must have been the mill cottages. The one right at the river's edge drew my attention: a little path from the cottage door led right on to the river, and there in the water were four or five big stones – these I would imagine were stepping-stones, so that the inhabitants could dip their buckets into the river to get their water, their only source for many, many years. I looked back at the mill, a huge solid building of rich honey-coloured Cotswold stone. At one time there were at least three mills in Bourton, and up until 1949 this one was still working. Between then and 1978 it was used for a number of different things. Now it is a most wondrous motor museum and a 'must' for every visitor. A man called Mike Cavanagh saw the potential of the lovely building, and in 1978 he bought it: now it houses a number of vintage cars and automobilia. He has a collection of over 600 period advertising signs, and hundreds and hundreds of items from pre-war days – there's a complete 1920 motor cycle workshop; a blacksmith's forge with all the old tools; toys and household things; and an old-fashioned village shop. Mike Cavanagh told me that years ago a Mr Preece, who made motor bikes in Coventry, made one called *The Windrush*, because his wife came from that area; but he hadn't one of those models.

In a small road off the High Street I found a big, old Cotswold house, its outside covered with built-in stone nest holes for pigeons or doves: another reminder of the past when men were glad to 'house' these birds.

Out along the village (or is it a town?) main street again, the Windrush has taken on a completely new look – no reeds or rushes or loosestrife, but a wide, tidy, softly flowing river, with stone-built banks and broad tree-lined grass lawns. The river through Bourton is spanned by five lovely stone-arched bridges that link the main street to the side streets and to the riverside, where thousands and thousands of visitors flock yearly. There is much to attract them – a wonderful model village (an exact replica of Bourton), Birdland, a model railway, a perfumery, and dozens and dozens of shops, cafés and hotels to cater for the needs of the visitors. And, always, there is the Windrush, where people can just sit on the bank and enjoy the sunshine and the water, or feed the numerous ducks that swim up and down the river waiting for titbits.

On one side of the Windrush, lovely stone-built houses line the banks: at this time of year their gardens were bright with autumn flowers and foliage. And every tree along the grass verge was proudly showing its autumn colour: hues of wine, brilliant red, bright yellow to honey colour and copper beech brown. Some of the leaves from the sycamores and limes were already fallen, and I scuffed my feet through them, disturbing the lovely, leafy, autumnal smell. From there I made my way out of Bourton, to a super trout farm and the car park, and then on to the outskirts of the village, where the river Dickler joins the ever-winding Windrush.

Pigeons' paradise in Sherborne Street, Bourton-on-the-Water

One of the elegant bridges at Bourton

I t was a typical November day when I set out for my next journey along the Windrush valley. The fog lay thick everywhere, like a blanket blotting out the landscape. But the forecast was that it would clear towards mid-morning, so I felt quite hopeful. An old Gloucester man used to say about foggy days: 'It wraps round yu', and that's how I felt – shrouded in it. Everything around me was enveloped in it, with houses suddenly rearing up in front, and ghost-like footsteps of someone whom I couldn't see on the

other side of the road. And it was quite cold, raw cold: of this type of day my old shepherd friend used to say, 'The only place I sweats today is at the nose ind.' [end]

Towards eleven o'clock the fog began to move. At first I could just see the tops of the trees and a church tower, then quite suddenly the sun broke through, shafting through the trees, lighting up the cottages, fields and countryside. Every bush, twig and branch was laced with hundreds of cobwebs, each hung with pearl-drops of mist. To my left a large wood glowed, golden with larch trees – larch is the only conifer which loses its spikes or needles, as they are often called, in the autumn. In the spring they are a wonderful fresh green; now in November they look like a thread of gold running through the wood. The oaks still had their leaves on – they must be the last of our trees to lose them. But at this time of the year most of the firs and conifers come into their own, and show up glossy and dark green in the woods.

Traveller's Joy

Just on the edge of the wood I could pick out the lovely pink and orange berries of the spindle bush – the hard wood was used at one time for the making of spindles for cloth and blanket weaving; another use for the wood was for meat skewers. I like to pick a few sprays to take indoors, to brighten up the place during the dark days of November. And here and there the trees and bushes were draped with Old Man's Beard, the grey seed-heads of the wild clematis, or Traveller's Joy as it is more often called. In the hedges sprays of scarlet hips glowed bright alongside the rich dark red haw berries (fruit of the May bush), which we always called 'azzies' when we were young. Come the end of the year, or early January, all the berries will have been greedily eaten by the winter-visiting birds, like the fieldfares (velts, my husband used to call them), along with redwing and woodcock and many others. One elderly neighbour of mine used to say, about this time of the year, 'Ah, missus, my northern thrush 'ull be showing up any day now. He sets up in that tree and sings all winter long. You want to hear him when the weather's going to be bad, I wonder he don't burst his windpipe.' What I think she was referring to was probably a missel-thrush, but because it was winter-time with not many birds singing, she evidently noticed it more. Mind you, we always refer to them as storm cocks.

My first call today was the village of Sherborne – again, not strictly on the Windrush. Sherborne is a well planned village, the cottages early Victorian with nice long front gardens which are very pleasing to the eye. It has its own 'Sherborne Brook' which glides into the Windrush just outside the village. I have a great love for the place, for it was here that my grandparents, uncles and aunts lived, and my mother, until her marriage; during my younger days I stayed often with one or another of my relatives, and went to the village school there for a while. At one period I had been despatched to my aunt and uncles there because my mother, left a widow with four children some three years earlier, was about to be married again (this I learned later), and I suspect it was thought that as the youngest I might find the intrusion of a man into the home a bit difficult to accept. After a year at Sherborne I began to behave rather badly, I think because I was missing my home and family, and my aunt apparently wrote and told my mother of this. One day I was walking home from school with my cousins, bawling my head off for one reason or another, when along the road

Fieldfare, a winter visitor

came a lady riding a bicycle. She dismounted and through my tears I recognised my mother, who had ridden on an old bike she had borrowed, all the way from Ducklington – a matter of about twenty miles – to fetch me home. The hugging and the kissing soon dried my tears. I remember the discomfort of sitting on the tin carrier at the back of her bicycle on the journey, but that didn't matter – I was going home! – to find that my mother had produced a new little baby sister. At first, they all thought that I would be jealous, but no, I loved her, and was happy in the fact that I was home at last.

Sherborne today is a lovely, quiet village, but centuries ago Sherborne Manor belonged to Winchcombe Abbey, and in the spring thousands of their sheep were washed in Sherborne Brook, and shorn on the banks, providing work for the locals for a few weeks. The village, situated so near the London Road and the wool centre at nearby Northleach, was quite handy for transporting the wool to the city.

The present Sherborne House, built in 1850 and now made into luxury flats, is hardly visible from the road as it is surrounded by a great high wall. My grandfather was employed on the estate as shepherd, while my grandmother was gate-opener. They lived in one of the lodge cottages on the now busy A40 (then called the London Road, of course). For her job my grandmother was paid sixpence a week. My mother used to tell us of how the 'Big House' was

The Post Office, Sherborne

supposedly haunted by Crump Dutton, a one-time owner, and on this foggy November day, when I visited the village, one could easily imagine ghosts lurking about the great passages of Sherborne House.

I called and had a good chat with Mr and Mrs Taylor, who for many years ran the village shop and Post Office there – as did his parents, to whom I used to deliver groceries during the War when I drove a wholesale grocer's lorry. We spoke of Crump Dutton's ghost, and Mr

Taylor agreed there *was* something eerie about the place – he had felt it, and so had others in the village.

In the beech trees opposite the Taylors' cottage, families of rooks were gathering and chattering; this meeting was not to reserve their old nesting place for the spring, but just to congregate and talk over last summer's goings-on – at least, it is said that this is what happens at this time of the year.

As I made my way out of Sherborne I noticed a cottage with a beautifully carved Norman doorway; was this a relic of the earlier Sherborne Manor, I wondered. I reached the point where the Sherborne Brook joins the Windrush; from there it meanders along through meadowland until it reaches the village which is named after the river – Windrush, which lies on a hill above the river. On a small green here, the lime trees had lost all their leaves. Nearby is the church of St Peter with a cluster of Cotswold stone cottages opposite. At the church gate there is an old stone mounting-block, a reminder of the days when the farmers and landowners rode to church on horseback, sometimes bringing their wives riding pillion. The church is very lovely, with a beautifully carved Jacobean pulpit. Along the main aisle lie the tombstones of some of my

Windrush church

forebears, the name BROAD carved on almost all of them. But the most fascinating feature is the south doorway, which is Norman and has a double row of carved beak-heads, every one different from the next: these carvings go right down to the jambs and are very unusual. In the churchyard there are lots of lovely carved tombstones, the work a reminder of the stone masons who once lived thereabouts.

Today Windrush is a quietly beautiful place, but was once a hive of local workers, probably because of the well-known oolite stone quarry nearby which helped to provide material for some of the lovely buildings in London and Oxford, and many other places.

Below the village the softly flowing Windrush slips beneath a veil of thickets and reeds as it winds its way through wooded coombes until it reaches Great Barrington. Here the river divides into two separate streams, because of the mills that once stood on the banks, but about a mile and a half downstream, at Little Barrington, it unites again. From the Fox Inn at the crossroads I first made my way to Great Barrington, crossing over the two river bridges. As I reached the last one I heard a loud screaming and squealing, and looking to where the noise was coming from I saw that a stoat had just caught a rabbit. The captor held its victim down, and the poor rabbit was squirming and struggling, its white bobby tail visible now and then. Then the struggle and the noise ceased, and the stoat, with its black tail tip showing, dragged his prey off into a group of weeds growing by the river's edge – to enjoy his dinner, no doubt. I

walked up the hill, where the walls surrounding the Great Park at this point were several feet high. I passed the church (I could call there on my way back) then went on past the great gates of the Mansion and off to my left. I wanted to see if the deer in the Park were still visible

Stoat – enemy of the rabbit

from a small side road. I looked through the great rusting wrought-iron gates: yes! they were still there, grazing in the Park. I could also see a lovely summerhouse, but not the Mansion, from there.

Great Barrington village was very quiet and a bit disappointing. Some of the cottages were empty and some in a ruinous state, and there seemed very few people about. I did see a couple of men loading up something or other in a big farmyard surrounded by great, grey barns. I walked along a back road; here were a solid stone-built deserted village hall and a biggish school, but no sign of life at all. Further down the road I saw a woman hanging her washing out. 'That won't dry today, missus,' I called out, smiling. 'I know it won't,' she replied, 'but I do like to let it have a blow.' 'Why is everything so quiet and neglected here?' I enquired; she just shrugged her shoulders and walked into her cottage: but I understand that many of the cottages are soon to be modernised.

Then, as I walked up the main street, I heard the clanging sound of metal on metal. Could it be a blacksmith's forge in this very quiet place, I wondered. Sure enough, in an ancient Cotswold building that has been a blacksmith's shop since 1879 I found three generations of the Hall family working: Mr Bill Hall, who started working there for his father in 1926 for £1 a week; his son, Brian, who joined his father in 1954; and *his* son, David, who came straight from school to work in the family business.

The 'stable' door was one of those cut straight across the middle, so that if you wish, the bottom half can be kept shut while the upper half is flung open. Outside, set in the stone wall, I noticed that there were several iron rings. They would have been used to tether impatient horses – cart horses, ponies and hunters – while they waited to be shod.

Inside the forge the walls were hung with blacksmithing tools – huge, long-handled tongs, hammers and things, all rusty and dusty, but no longer in daily use. The forge fire glowed red and warm. 'It's the same old fire that was put in when my grandfather worked here,' Bill Hall told me. 'Mind you, we don't blow it up with *them* these days,' he went on as he pointed to a great pair of bellows which stood in the corner. 'Now it's electrically powered, saves a lot of time and energy. He flicked a switch and in minutes the fire became a red, roaring bed of heat. All the time Bill was filing a piece of metal, though I never got down to asking him what it was. I was loath to leave the dark, warm building. The atmosphere and the darkness of the blacksmith's shop reminded me of a blacksmith who had a smithy a few miles from my home. One day, Fred Coggins slipped in there for a chat. It was a dull old day, so Fred remarked to Amos, the blacksmith, 'By jingo, thas dark in yer, Amos. I wunder you don't have a bit of a skylight in the roof.' 'Well,' Amos replied, 'If I dun that the kids 'ud throw stones up and break it.' 'Well,' Fred said, 'you could always chuck a sack over it, couldn't yer?'

Outside in the cold air, I found Brian busy welding, making a big balcony rail. He had to work at it outside as it was far too big a project to fit into the smithy. He told me, 'This is the sort of thing we do these days; 'course, we still mend quite a lot of farm machinery, too, but most big farms have their own workshops, and a farm worker has to be able to turn his hand at mending and repairing some of the machinery these days.'

Meanwhile, young David was busy blacking a lovely wrought-iron fire basket that they had made for a local person. 'They just pop in,' Brian told me, when I asked him about the design, 'with a sort of rough pencil drawing along with the measurements, and then we produce this sort of thing.

Great Barrington church

I wonder if they'd get that sort of treatment in the big stores in the city,' he added.

And although the village seemed almost deserted – apart from the black-smith's – the church of St Mary the Virgin was beautifully looked after, the flowers were fresh and bright and it had an air of caring about it. On one wall there is an exquisitely embroidered picture by the late Lady Winfield, depicting Mary and the baby Jesus, and just inside the door is a marble group showing two children of the Bray family who died of smallpox in 1711. Another monument, again for a member of the Bray family, is that of Captain Edmund Bray of Barrington Park. He is dressed in Tudor style and has his sword by his right side. Was he left-handed? Or is there some truth in the story that he once killed a man, but was pardoned by Queen Elizabeth I and thereafter wore his sword on the right so that he would be unable to use it again?

On my way to Little Barrington, great yew trees on the edge of the Park dominated the road-side. Yew trees are usually found only in churchyards, as they are poisonous to cattle and cattle don't graze in churchyards; at one time the trees were grown in England to provide wood for the making of bows – when bows and arrows were used in battle.

At Little Barrington village, the winter sun shone on the cottages and the lichen on the roof slates sparkled golden and

Cotswold cottages at Little Barrington

green. Here, most of the cottages are built around a large green hollow, from which, it is said, the stone actually came to build them. Each dwelling is delightfully different from its neighbour, characteristic of the truly Cotswold stones and slates. Still standing are two old pumps, one at each end of the row of cottages; from these the inhabitants would once have got their water. On one doorway are the words 'Post Office', just a small cottage with a stone seat on either side of the porch but, however small, at least the folk here *have* a Post Office, which is more than they have at Great Barrington. In the green hollow a small spring flows out of the hillside and eventually over a field and into the Windrush. It was in that hollow, during the War, I used to gather the watercress which grew in great abundance there. I had to stop just opposite the little spring to take goods in to a Mr Hayward who kept the village shop; but that has been closed long since.

I glanced up the road; an elderly man with a jet-black dog by his side came walking towards me. Here, I thought, is someone who I could possibly have a chat to about this charming place. Friendly good-mornings were said, and I told the man (John Harris) that I was writing a book about the Windrush and the places along its banks. I asked him where he lived. 'Down Minnow Lane,' he replied – and what a picture that conjured up! But it was just the sort of place I wanted to see, as he said it led straight to the river.

'You'll find it just beyond the church,' he said, 'up that road there.' And off he went with his dog.

Apart from a farm tractor or two, the place was fairly quiet, and yet years ago both Great and Little Barrington were quite important places because of the local stone-quarries. The Strong family who lived nearby were famous master masons; one, Thomas Strong, was asked by Christopher Wren to lay the foundation stone of St Paul's Cathedral, London, and other members of the family also helped in its building. The stone from the quarries was shipped from here and other Windrush villages in great, flat-bottomed barges, down the river Windrush, then on to the Thames, and eventually to London. On the Windrush here, near the village, can still be seen part of a sloping weir: here, it is said, the water level could be raised so that the heavily-laden barges could avoid the mill race.

I walked up the hill and almost out of the village, to the church of St Peter, a very different building from the churches I had seen on my journey so far. It is quite small, with a squat tower, but it is a friendly little place with a Norman doorway, and on the outside of the porch is a piece of sculpture, easily overlooked, of two couples, the women in long dresses and the men in very old-fashioned clothes. This piece is said to be in memory of a family called Taylers, who once lived there.

A bit further along the road I came to a lane – Minnow Lane. The road was not very well made up, but on one side was a row of stone cottages leading down to the Windrush. The cottages belong to a charity run by the village, and most of the folk I saw were elderly. At the end there was no road right back to the village, but just a pathway – to save people going all the way round. Again, a little way along the road was another lane. I had been told that there were remains of a paper mill down there, but the property appeared to be privately-owned, so I didn't venture. I could see a sort of slatted building at the end; these slats were supposed to be where the 'vellum'

was dried before being written on. This, it seems, is all that is left of a once busy paper-making mill.

I took a pleasant, very narrow, side road where deep in the valley the Windrush winds in several great loops across open meadows, with hills on either side, as it makes its way towards the hamlet of Upton, which stands on high ground above the river and about half a mile from Burford town. Folk say that it was near here centuries ago that an important battle was fought: in fact, there's a field still known locally as 'Battle Edge'. It was a furious conflict of hand-to-hand fighting with cudgels, axes and swords between the men of Mercia and those of Wessex which raged over the river Windrush. In the end the

men of Wessex won, and still the people of Burford celebrate this victory, with a huge golden dragon wending its way through the town at midsummer.

I wandered down a muddy lane towards the Windrush, where a large wooden bridge for farm machinery spanned the river. I stood and watched the swirling water for a while. Suddenly a kingfisher flashed by, time enough for me to see the brilliant blue of this shy bird – truly a jewel on this cold November day.

Down there I saw too the remains of what, many years ago, had been Burford's bathing pool. Now all that is left are a few short posts sticking up in the river, and lumps of rotten wood that must have been shelters where people used to change into their bathing costumes. But I wondered why the pool was built so far away from the town. Perhaps it was because the river at this point was wide and deep – something to do with the fact that once, years ago, yet another mill stood nearby. Besides relying on Windrush water to work the mill wheels, what a lot of people must have relied on the river for their living by working in those mills, whether paper, cloth, weaving or corn mills.

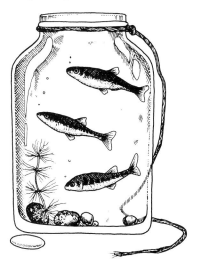

Now the mist, rising up from the river, had become quite thick – so thick that I could hardly make out the hills beyond. Time I made for home.

Down Minnow Lane

A cold and frosty morning on Burford Hill

But I would be where Windrush sweet
Leaves Burford's lovely hill
The grey old town on lonely down
Is where I would be still.

H.C. Beeching

Beautiful Burford, 'the town on the hill', as it is so often described, is not lonely any more, for tourists from all over the world flock to this delightful Cotswold town all the year round.

I usually make my way off the busy A40 when I get into Burford, and pause for a few minutes and gaze at the town from there — there is no other view quite like it. The tree-lined road drops quickly and steeply. On either side of the road, from top to bottom, there is the most wonder-

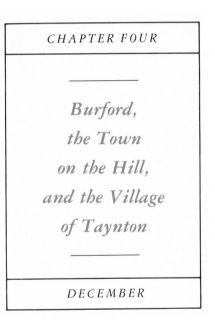

CHAPTER FOUR

Burford,
the Town
on the Hill,
and the Village
of Taynton

DECEMBER

ful variety of small cottages, elegant houses, ancient hotels, inns and shops to be found, all dating from the thirteenth century onwards. Each building is different from its neighbour, with roofs of varying levels but all tiled with Cotswold slates, and built of Cotswold stone, some with mullioned windows and drip-stones, and old carved doorways. The stone was mostly quarried locally from Burford, Taynton or Upton quarries. The town is still surrounded by fields

Old mill on Windrush side

and lush green rolling uplands, and is a tourist's paradise. Yet the river Windrush which flows at the bottom of the hill does not really interest the tourist. Oh yes, visitors walk as far as the ancient bridge, with its little bays so that pedestrians can stand safe from the continuous flow of traffic and gaze at the softly flowing ever-winding river. From the bridge they can see the willow trees standing drunkenly on either side of the river bank, but that's it. I wonder whether Burford makes enough of the Windrush? But then, they have their famous hill.

Of course, it was a very different story many years ago, when the mills – there were two, not counting the one at nearby Upton – stood on the Windrush bank.

Just over the bridge is where the first mill was worked. The buildings are still there, grey and solid as ever. For nine hundred years – so the present owner told me – the mill ground corn into flour for the townsfolk. During the latter part of its life, from about 1876 until 1980, it was machine-driven and it pumped water, not directly from the Windrush but from a spring on a hillside along the Taynton road, up to a reservoir in Burford: this was the town's supply for one hundred years. The meadow where the spring is can easily be recognised as it is very often flooded, the water from it eventually flowing into the Windrush close to the mill. The mill's weir is still there and on the day that I called, in late December, after we had had rather a lot of rain, the water was rushing through the weir and then swirling around a bend at a terrific rate. Mr Mills, the owner of the buildings, hopes one day to have the engine that drove the mill working again.

From here the Windrush flows under the ancient bridge past the seclusion of private gardens before it reaches the other mill in Witney Street. In the time of Henry VIII this was a fulling and tucking mill, then later it became a mill for cloth-weaving. In the nineteenth century it was a flour mill, and in the first part of the twentieth century housed Burford Laundry. But now, in the 1980s, it has been tastefully restored and converted to holiday apartments – with the river still flowing underneath the main building.

The town has much to offer, and it is steeped in history. There is the lovely church of St John the Baptist, with its tall elegant spire. Inside there are many elaborate tombs and memorials to the folk of long ago who helped to build the town. The grandest tomb in there must be that of Sir Lawrence and Lady Tanfield; both were most unpopular in Burford because of their devious goings-on during their lifetime there. The pair realised they were hated by the community, and it is said that Lady Tanfield was once heard to remark that she 'would like to grind the people of Burford to powder beneath the wheels of her chariot'.

And it was in a fiery chariot that she was supposed to have haunted the people of Burford by riding over the roofs of the town in it, sometimes accompanied by Sir Lawrence. In the eighteenth century the chariot ridings became so frequent that a band of clergy – some say it was four, others seven – met with bell, book and candle to 'lay her ghost'. The story goes that the holy men cajoled her into a bottle. They corked this very tightly and then threw it into the river Windrush, just under the third arch of the bridge. Local folk once believed that if, in

Goldfinch

times of drought, the Windrush just under the third arch should run dry, then Lady Tanfield would start her meanderings over the rooftops again. And *many* years ago, during a severe drought, some of the inhabitants took buckets of water along to avert this happening.

Also in the church, on the lead surrounding the beautiful font, are scratched these words: 'Anthony Sedley, Prisner: 1649' – a reminder of when some of

Cromwell's Levellers mutinied. Cromwell and Fairfax caught up with them at Burford, capturing about three hundred and forty and locking them in the church – the only building big enough to hold them. Some were shot the next day and buried in the churchyard. Outside, in the churchyard, there are several huge gravestones called 'bale tombs', the tops of them resembling rolled-up blankets or cloth – a reminder of the Cotswold wool trade that was prominent in the area. These cavernous gravestones came in very handy for the men who poached deer in nearby Wychwood Forest; they would lift a great heavy lid and hide the venison in there out of sight of the gamekeeper. Then, when the coast was clear, the meat was taken to their homes. It was said at the time that the labourers of Burford ate more venison in a year than London's gentry. But these days the churchyard is a beautiful peaceful place, with the gravestones and the surrounding walls covered in lichens, white and silver, gold and green, which gleam in the sunlight.

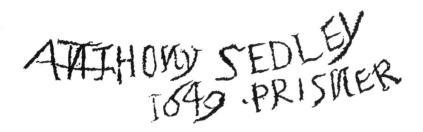

In the High Street is the famous fourteenth century Tolsey, where the tolls were once collected: now the upstairs is used as a local museum. And at the bottom of the hill, close to the river on the right-hand side, there is a lovely old gabled house: look closely and you can read what is inscribed on it:

Symon Wysdom Alderman
The First Founder of the schole
in Burford gave thes Tenements
With Other to the same schole
In A.N. 1577 and newly reedyfyed
And buylded the same in A.N. 1576·
All Lawde and prayse be given
To God ther fore. Amen.

As this is a book about the river Windrush, I must not go on about the history of Burford: there are already plenty of books on that subject! But there is one story that is not so well known as most.

Early in the eighteenth century a lady called Mrs Huntley started to bake biscuits at the school, where she was Matron and her husband was the schoolmaster. She also sold the biscuits to the stage-coach passengers who alighted nearby. Sons and grandsons and great grandsons of Mrs Huntley continued making and selling biscuits, and in 1841 one, Thomas Huntley, went into partnership with a George Palmer – so began the very successful world famous biscuit-makers, Huntley and Palmer, now of Reading.

The next day I set out along a pleasant country road to visit the nearby village of Taynton. There had been a sharp frost overnight; it was a real winter's day with the air clear and bracing, and with quite bright sunshine. A few blackbirds were chacketing in the hedges – then suddenly I heard a different sound: some of the migrant fieldfares and redwings had arrived! About three or four dozen flew low over my head to land on a good thick hedge of hawthorn bushes, rich red with hawberries. Such a chatter and commotion as they landed, but what I would call a happy sound. They were evidently glad to find such a feast after their long journey. There is a good crop of berries everywhere along this part of the Windrush valley, so they should be all right for food for some time. Out in the field there were quite a few pheasants feeding, the cocks showing up so brilliantly on the white, frosty grass. Whenever I see pheasants they always remind me of what once happened to one of my brothers when he went off

poaching. It was a very cold, rimey, frosty night and bright moonlight too. He said to my mum, 'I'm off to get a long tailed 'un (a cock pheasant). They'll be roosting on the branches on a night like this. Shan't be long.' Well, he walked a couple of miles down to a small plantation where there were always plenty of pheasants. He crept into the thickly wooded area and hadn't gone far when he spied a beauty perched quite low. Quietly, with arms outstretched, he walked towards it, when a gruff voice behind him said, 'What's the bloody game, then?' Without even a backward glance my brother dived into the Windrush and up the bank the other side, before the keeper could get his breath or recognise him. When he

Memorials to wool merchants

Winter rabbit

Busy blackbird

arrived home he was frozen stiff and white with rimey frost. A quick swabble down with a kettle of hot water (no bathroom in those days) and off to bed with a hot flat-iron wrapped in a bit of blanket to warm him, and in the morning he was no worse for his cold ducking.

The next night my stepfather went down to the local for his usual half-pint. The keeper was in there telling a tale to one of the villagers. 'Saw the bloody funniest thing last night. I was out in Flexy Wood, looking out for poachers – proper poacher's moon last night, it was – when I suddenly comes across this bloke. I reckon he was just about to pluck one of the gaffer's birds off a low lying branch. So I creeps up behind him and asks him what he's up to, and the fool dived straight into the river and up the other side and ran off like a bloody gazelle. And you know how cold that was. I should think the poor bugger's in bed with pneumonia tonight.'

Along the roadside a couple of grey squirrels were scratching and searching for beechnuts amongst the fallen leaves. They are inclined to hide their findings away, and then when they need them cannot remember where they are hidden. In the hedge I noticed a snowberry bush with white transparent berries on it (snotty gozzles, we called them as children: press one between the finger and thumb and you will know why we called them this!). The frost overnight will soon put paid to *those* berries.

I reached the village of Taynton,

Greedy grey squirrel

Cottages from local stone, Taynton

one of the loveliest along the Windrush valley; well, it's not strictly on the
Windrush side, but very close, and it happens to be the first Oxfordshire village
near the river. There was a flour mill here long long ago, but it ceased working
in the 1930s. Now it forms part of a beautiful house. But the sluice gate
remains, and every year the dipper bird comes back to breed on the Windrush
there.

Today the village is very quiet; just a few cottages, the lovely church of St
John the Evangelist, and two or three farms. One of these, along with its group
of farm buildings, is in what must be the most wonderful setting anywhere in
the Cotswolds – stone and slate, slate and stone, nothing more wondrous
anywhere. And all local stone, too, because for 900 years 'freestone' was quarried
here. To this day, Taynton still has its quarry, but it is not now used
commercially, though the owner, Mr Philip Lee, still works it in a very small
way, and his knowledge of stone and stone quarries is remarkable; he can tell
you everything there is to know about the lovely warm yellow oolite.

When Vanburgh built Blenheim Palace early in the eighteenth century, he

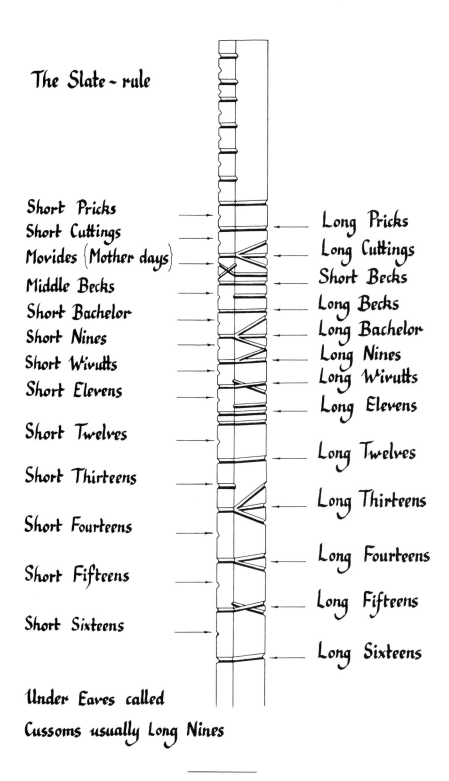

The Slate - rule

Short Pricks
Short Cuttings
Movides (Mother days)
Middle Becks
Short Bachelor
Short Nines
Short Wivutts
Short Elevens

Short Twelves

Short Thirteens

Short Fourteens

Short Fifteens

Short Sixteens

Long Pricks
Long Cuttings
Short Becks
Long Becks
Long Bachelor
Long Nines
Long Wivutts
Long Elevens

Long Twelves

Long Thirteens

Long Fourteens

Long Fifteens

Long Sixteens

Under Eaves called
Cussoms usually Long Nines

Barley Cob

insisted that only Taynton freestone was to be used, and in 1938 when the new Bodleian Library was built in Oxford, the stone came from the Taynton quarry. Some of Oxford's most famous buildings, including Christ Church Cathedral, were mostly built from the Taynton freestone.

What tales the hollows and the hummocks on the high ground above the village could tell, from the time when the quarries were busy with masons, and shouting, sweating men loading those huge blocks of stone, and the horses strained under the heavy loads. Only the names in the churchyard remind us of what a busy, bustling place Taynton once was. Several of the gravestones bear the name of Pittaway, masons and stoneworkers. I wonder, was that name born from the primitive tool used for centuries by slate and stone workers, a pick attached to a wooden handle: one thing it was used for was to 'peck' or 'pick' a peghole in roofing slates (i.e. picking away or pecking away); or does it come from the pit-pat sound made by the man as he worked?

It is interesting to hear the old names of the slates, too. There are twenty-six different ones, named according to their size: Wivutts, short and long; Bachelors, long nines and short nines; Cussoms and Movides, are just a few. And the men would use a long measuring stick, when they were roofing buildings, marked with notches which only old roofers could read.

I found a delightful little booklet in the church, and in it you can read all about the village. A lovely old custom was once held in Taynton Church on St Thomas's

Burford Bridge

Day, called The Barley Cob Charity – a bread charity – and these were the rules:

A quarter of barley meal was provided annually to be grown at *Sherborne*, ground at *Windrush* mill, baked at *Barrington* Bakery and given to the poor children of *Burford* in *Taynton* Church, the loaves being known as Barley Clangers.

An old wall builder, as a small boy, had some of this fresh bread. 'But,' he said, 'I had to mek off quick, 'cos if I'd bin caught, I'd 'a' bin burforded [buffetted].' You see, he lived at the nearby village of Fulbrook, and the bread was only for Burford children.

From Burford town I made my way along the lower country road towards the village of Widford.

The bare top-most branches of the beech trees looked for all the world like delicate filigree work against the clear blue winter sky. That's one of the joyous things about winter-time – the glory of the bare branches; and I for one appreciate the trees' winter beauty, rather than the heavy leaf of summer. The whole vista was of windswept fields, with patches of rich

CHAPTER FIVE

'The river's always rippling as it runs beside the trees'

HENRY TAUNT

JANUARY

brown ploughing, and here and there the soft misty green of autumn-planted corn. In the meadows, away from the flooded fields of the Windrush valley, sheep grazed happily. Big flocks of rooks and jackdaws flew noisily overhead and a solitary robin sang to me from a hazel bush. Before the coming of the A40 it was along this lower road that horse-drawn coaches lumbered – as many as thirty a day – as they travelled to and fro on the London–Gloucester run.

I wandered along the country road, with the ever-winding river just a field away to my left. Suddenly I had a surprise: there, blowing in the wind, was a bush of early catkins, dancing and sprinkling their gold-dust to pollinate the tiny red-tufted female flowers on their own branches.

I reached the village of Widford, and crossed over the bridge where, of course, yet another mill once stood, which in its time had been first a fulling mill, then

On the way to Widford

Widford church

a corn mill; its last task was to saw up timber when many trees on the estate were felled. Now the buildings are made into attractive houses.

Widford is often described as 'the deserted village', and in the field where the very small, lovely, lonely church of St Oswald's stands are hummocks and small hillocks. In the fourteenth century there was a small community of thirteen houses there, clinging close to the church. Was it the Black Death that struck this lovely place, leaving only the church, the mill and the manor and manor farm buildings, and a shepherd's cottage in a field, and the humps and the hillocks and the cold January wind whistling through the brown dried grasses? But the little church in the field is certainly worth a visit, and has a delightful charm all its own. It dates back to the early twelfth century and is built on the site of a Roman villa; in the chancel there is evidence of this, in the form of some Roman paving. On the walls are some very interesting fourteenth-century murals, and the old high-backed pews, complete with doors, are eighteenth century.

From the church I took a very pleasant field walk to the village of Swinbrook, the next place along the Windrush valley. I wanted to see where for four centuries the wealthy family of the Fettiplaces had lived, in a beautiful manor house, with wonderful gardens and fish-ponds. Now all that is left of the glorious place is a terraced field on a hillside and the remains of some ponds. But in the church of St Mary there are six marble figures of the Fettiplaces: they lie reclining in two tiers of three shelves, poised as if waiting for something. Three are Tudor gentlemen and the other three are dressed in the Stuart style. An old jingle from that period describes how very wealthy the family was:

> The Tracys, the Lacys and the Fettiplaces
> Own all the woods, the parks and places.

By the early nineteenth century all the male side of the family had died out, and the estate was divided up. The Fettiplace mansion was eventually let to a London gentleman, a Mr Freeman, a charming, respectable man who had many servants and kept open house to the gentry, his friendship much sought-after by the surrounding rich families. Soon after he arrived, however, highway robberies became quite frequent, especially along the Gloucester road, where the stage-coaches were frequently held up. Then the robberies began to take place further afield, sometimes on the London to Banbury road, and the Worcester to London road. These hold-ups went on for over a year; sometimes it was just a single highwayman, and sometimes it was a gang of four or five. Then one day the gang made an attack on a stage-coach that was well guarded. One of the guards surprised the highwaymen by holding them up with a pistol before they could make their usual demands. The gang, realising that they had been caught out, made off, but not before one of them had been very badly wounded and couldn't mount his horse. It was dear, respectable Mr Freeman's butler. The villagers of Swinbrook were horrified when the Bow Street Runners arrived and arrested – among others – the tenant of the manor, Mr Freeman, who in fact was a well-known highwayman whom the Bow Street Runners had been trying to catch for years.

The beautiful mansion in the Windrush valley never recovered from this dreadful happening, and the house was left empty, soon fell into ruin, and crumbled away. The stones were carted off for building in and around the village, but some of the stained glass windows from the mansion eventually went to the village church of St James at Stonesfield in Oxfordshire. Apparently some of the armorial shields which had been in the windows at Swinbrook passed to the famous collector of antiquities, Alderman William Fletcher of Oxford and Yarnton, and from him to his nephew, Thomas Robinson, whose country house was at Begbroke in Oxfordshire. In 1827 Robinson employed Thomas Willement, an expert in stained glass, to glaze the windows of Begbroke Church, and some of the Fettiplace shields were used for this purpose. But they were removed by the Reverend Francis Robinson (Rector of Stonesfield 1834–1886) to his village church; so although the village of Stonesfield, a few miles from Swinbrook, had no previous connection with the Fettiplace family, yet the church has become the home of the remaining Fettiplace armorial shields, and is one of the most important collections of heraldic glass of the early Tudor period to be found in the county. The ordinary observer can recognise the Fettiplace arms – gules, two chevrons azure (a red shield carrying two silver chevrons) – where they mark the marriages between this and other great families.

But the Fettiplaces will never be forgotten, because of the six marble effigies in the church and the fact that Sir George, the last in the male line, left charity money: first, to provide bread for the poor; second, to provide seven green overcoats for seven poor men; and, third, the monies to send two poor boys to Christ's Hospital to learn to be medical men. These days the charity provides help with electricity bills for pensioners who need it, and help with education and equipment, etc., to local

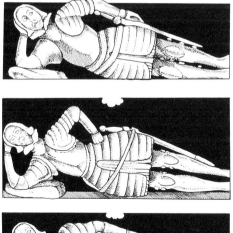

schools in the parish. Although for many years no one took advantage of the Christ's Hospital offer, one young person has just completed his training there, and another just started. The Reverend Timothy Hind, the Vicar of Asthall, Swinbrook and Widford, told me that up until the last war the green coats were still being provided, and that the bread charities only ended in the 1960s.

Swinbrook is indeed a lovely village, with a small bubbling stream running through it which eventually flows into the Windrush further down the street – which is lined with delightful Cotswold stone cottages and houses, and beautifully tended gardens with springs tumbling out of the rolling hillsides and surrounded by green fields and wooded valleys – all typical of the Cotswolds. It is the freestone and limestone that help to bring such loveliness to Cotswold buildings, and of course the stone walls which run for miles here. They are covered in white and silver-reddish and brown lichen and are most attractive. The mildness of the weather had brought some of the moss which also grows over the walls out in minute flowers. On the afternoon I was there, the winter sun shone on them, making the tiny flowers glow rich and red. It was here that for some time after the First World War, Lord Redesdale and his wife and family lived in the beautiful manor house, after moving from nearby Asthall Manor. His daughters were the famous Mitford girls. I remember one day, years ago, before the last war, when I was shopping in the nearby town of Witney: suddenly a huge car with the hood down drew up just opposite where I was standing. Out of it tripped four or five of the most gorgeous, attractive, beautifully-dressed girls that I ever saw – either before or since. They were the Mitford girls. I just stood there open-mouthed at these happy, laughing young ladies, as they wandered into what was then the nicest dress shop in the town. This was, of course, before the time of Unity Mitford's most unfortunate friendship with Hitler, which ended so tragically. She now lies buried in the quiet beautiful churchard of St Mary's, with her sister Nancy.

Swinbrook, village in a valley

Old mill and Swan Inn, Swinbrook

Near the church is the Swan Inn, standing alongside the old mill with the Windrush flowing under a delightful stone bridge. One old fellow said to me, 'The Windrush is still running, but it does no work now.' Not in the way that he remembers, perhaps, but the Thames Water Board draws from it to help fill the reservoirs at nearby Worsham, and the day I was visiting the area my companion took me to Kitesbrook Farm, now two cottages, whose residents still get their water supply from the Windrush, after it has gone through a filter. It is pumped up from the river by electricity. They also have a well in the garden which they can draw water from. All this is tested regularly, of course. I met one of the occupants, a charming 75-year-old Lithuanian, George, who works part-time on the estate, still rides his bike, and knows all there is to know about wood and trees. We were invited into his cottage for coffee and presented with a most beautiful flower arrangement, done by George, with flowers grown by him and watered with Windrush water: a truly remarkable man.

During the eighteenth century, in the nearby village of Fulbrook, just off the Windrush, there lived a most respectable family called Dunston. The story goes that three of the sons, Tom, Dick and Harry, began a life of crime which eventually brought two of them to the gallows. At first their wild escapades were confined to robbing local farmers of their stock and money when they went to and from market. They would hide the stolen animals in the Wychwood Forest, then, when the coast was clear, drive the animals miles away and sell them to unsuspecting farmers. The young men were very cunning and it is said they had their horses shod backwards so as to confuse would-be pursuers. Then they turned to holding up stage-coaches, sometimes working with other gangs and sometimes just the three of them. One night they rode out to Langley Hall, a few miles away; this was one of their hiding places, which they kept bolted and barred. Dick was the first to jump from his horse. He slipped his arm through the shutter on the door to open it, but a group of men were waiting inside and one grabbed Dick's arm and tied it to a bolt on the door, so that he couldn't get away. Realising that they might all be caught, Dick shouted to his brothers, 'Cut! Cut!' One of them drew his sword and severed Dick's arm at the elbow. His brothers dragged him onto his his horse and they galloped off into the night. Dick was never heard of again. It was thought he died of his injury and was buried secretly in Wychwood Forest.

But Tom and Harry were also soon to meet a terrible end. The year was 1767 and it was Burford's Whitsuntide Festival. Tom and Harry were playing cards at an inn at Capps Lodge, a lonely place outside the town where there was much drinking and squabbling. The landlord thought that the brothers were planning something, so when Harry got up to leave he followed him. Then all hell broke loose and there was shouting and shooting, and a tapster, William Harding, was very badly injured. The brothers were both held down on the floor, and eventually taken to Gloucester jail. A few weeks later William Harding died of his injuries and the Dunston brothers were charged with his murder and sentenced to death by hanging. Their bodies were encased in iron bands and then hanged on a gibbet on an oak tree near the edge of Wychwood Forest. For a long time afterwards people flocked for miles to see the bodies, which hung there for months covered with flies and with the birds pecking at them – a gruesome sight, and a terrible end. However, I understand that as a final act of defiance the brothers carved their initials and the date on that very gibbet tree where they were to hang. Just the other day I was taken to a field which was

Hangman's oak

Willows, like giant shaving brushes

once covered by the Wychwood Forest, and shown an old oak tree on its own in a field of beans. My companion said, 'The tree's looking a bit sick, see, the branches at the top are dead. Of course, it's a very old tree, but on no account would we chop it down. It will stay there until it falls!' I read the initials carved there – now, of course, rather distorted by time – H.D. and T.D. 1767 – and I gazed above at the huge thick heavy branch where the young men's lives had ended so tragically.

Away over a couple of fields is an old stone building, supposedly the rough old inn of Capps Lodge where gamblers and highwaymen met, and where the Dunston brothers were finally captured – there's even the remains of an old cock pit there, too.

On the walk to Asthall, the next village I was visiting, pollard willows lined the Windrush bank, their short branches ranging from palest yellow to gold, amber and red, their colours showing up brightly against the very blue winter sky. They looked for all the world like giant spiky shaving brushes.

The first thing that caught my eye on entering this charming unspoilt village were the handsome wrought iron gates of the beautiful Elizabethan manor house with its wide, elegant gables. The manor overlooks the lovely church of St Nicholas, which is certainly worth a visit, and a leaflet inside tells you much of the history. I was very interested in the chancel arch, which has Norman bird-beaking all around it; there are so many of them and all different. It is quite unusual to see beaking inside a church: normally it is used on the *outside*, as at Windrush village church. In the north chapel, under a decorated canopy, lies the figure of a lady in a wimple, veil and flowing dress, with a small lion-like animal at her feet. She is said to be Lady Joan Cornwall, wife of one Edmund Cornwall. There are many paintings on the walls and ceilings – the most that I have ever seen in one church. The manor was once owned by Edmund Cornwall.

Asthall lies on the Roman road of Akeman Street, and many Roman coins have been found there. My colleague and fellow 'Archer' Bob Arnold lived there when he was a youngster, and he told me that sometimes he picked up as many as a dozen Roman coins in a day, simply by walking along a freshly ploughed field. This started his interest in Roman coins, and when he sold his collection a few years ago, it was reckoned to be the finest in Great Britain. Mind you, only a small percentage of these coins were found at Asthall, and Bob's was a lifetime's collection.

The tree-lined green in the centre of the village looked cold and desolate on this winter's day. The wind cut like a knife, stinging my face, with flurries of hail, but I did pick a few sticky buds from a horse-chestnut tree there. In the warmth of my cottage they will soon be out, the crinkly leaves unfolding, looking like miniature palm trees, before the tiny 'candle' or flower comes into bloom. With so much rain the meadows right by the Windrush were flooded. I noticed that there were special 'holes' cut in a wall in front of a pond, so that flood water could flow through them, and that for several yards there were large flat stones on the wall near the river bridge. These were so that pedestrians could walk on the wall and onto the higher ground and then on the roadway over the bridge. This, of course, was when the roads used to flood badly, before the fields on the riverbank were properly drained. But the floods did not stop the swans – three pairs of them, all with their fawn-feathered children – gliding up the river. Soon

Sticky buds

the adults will be nesting and then the youngsters will be off, to turn into elegant swans themselves. A huge flock of starlings, hundreds of them, swept overhead, flying off to their roosting quarters; their acrobatic flight, just before they settle, is magnificent to watch.

The Windrush at Worsham

When the rains of early February at last stopped, I made my way towards Worsham, a small hamlet off the A4047 between Witney and Burford. As youngsters we always raced along past the signpost to Worsham, for fear of the legendary 'Black Stockings', a man who held up stage-coaches on dark windy nights, and who is still supposed to haunt that part of the old A40. Today the road is not quite as busy as it once was, for a bypass takes much of the

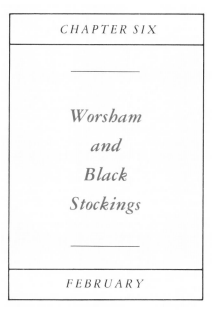

CHAPTER SIX

Worsham
and
Black
Stockings

FEBRUARY

fast-moving traffic on the London–Gloucester road. The view from the roadway is super: the Windrush valley with the river like a winding silver thread amongst the meadows, and the hills and the woods beyond, giving the traveller a glimpse of the Cotswold hills – in this part of the countryside the hills are smaller, but just as beautiful in their own way, for we are still in Cotswold country.

There were still large flocks of sheep, grazing on roots (mostly swede it looked like), but some were on grass, along with a few very early lambs. An old shepherd told me, 'Sheep does the ground a power of good, they treads the ground, yu see, as well as manuring it.' The weather was quite cold and wintry, with bitter easterly winds whipping across the hills and whistling through the bare branches of the trees. But the mild weather and rain of last month, along with a few days of quite warm sunshine, brought both flowers and foliage out far too soon – they probably think that spring is just around the corner, which it

isn't! Everywhere I've travelled this year in the Windrush area there seems to be a glut of snowdrops (Candlemas bells, we always called them), growing everywhere, on grassy banks well away from habitation, in gardens and orchards, churchyards and fields, masses and masses of them defying the cold winds and the few frosty nights that we have had. Several of the bushes and trees have awakened from their winter sleep: elder, honeysuckle and old man's beard are already showing tiny leaf buds, so too are some of the species of hawthorn, their brilliant green leaves showing up in the hedgerows. When we were children we called those first few tender green shoots 'bread and cheese', goodness knows why, and greedily grabbed them in handfuls and stuffed them in our ever-hungry mouths. I wonder now what it did for our stomachs! The wild white plum trees are out in full blossom, again blooming rather too early, so early that there are not many insects about to pollinate the flowers. This means a poor harvest of the fruit is inevitable.

The name Worsham is derived from Wulmarsham. Wulmer, it seems, was a presbyter of Edward the Confessor, and it is said that Wulmer once lived at Worsham. But, of course, the locals have always pronounced it as

'Oussham', referring to the dip and turn on the main road as 'Oussham Bottom', and it was here I made for on this wintry afternoon.

I walked down the steep hill towards Worsham. In the grass I spied a big clump of golden yellow coltsfoot, one of the earliest of the wild flowers to bloom. When we were young, in my neck of the woods we called them 'pee the beds', and we were frightened to pick them, in case we did just that – for a good hiding would have surely followed. And here and there in the hedge-bottom and on the grass verges, the fern-like leaves of cow parsley were showing. We always refer to the plant as 'keck', and for years people used to ask me why but I couldn't tell them. Recently I read that Shakespeare called it 'Kecksies', so that is probably where our name comes from.

I reached the mill, which like all the mills along the Windrush has a long history, as a fulling mill, a paper mill and then a corn mill; blankets were made there for many years, and during the First World War bell tents were manufactured there for the army. Mops, too, were produced from woolly material which was too coarse for blankets. Fairly recently a motor cycle firm used the mill buildings, and now a plastics firm is housed there making dustbins, buckets and bowls – products of our modern society. As well as the mill buildings, four houses and one bungalow make up the hamlet of Worsham.

Coltsfoot

I had arranged to meet Ann Cooper who was born in the cottage where she has lived all her life. She had promised to tell me all she knew about the legendary 'Black Stockings'.

'Well,' she said, as we stood outside her cottage, 'see that clump of willow trees over there? Look closely and you will see a stone building; it's what we call Old Lower Barn, and my mother told me that was where the man called "Black Stockings" lived.' We went into her cottage, warm and cosy, with a lovely blazing fire.

'This man,' she went on, 'who folk called "Black Stockings", was in fact a highwayman. But he had murdered someone at some time, either a stage-coach driver or a passenger, and of course, if he had been caught, they'd have hung him. So he stayed in the old barn all day, and then when night fell he'd climb up the steep bank in the field and get onto the road that way, holding up the stage-coaches and demanding money from the passengers. But he only came out on dark nights: well, if he'd ventured out on moonlight nights he might have been recognised. People spoke of seeing this furtive figure, dressed all in black so that he wouldn't show up, running across the London road. What finally became of him I never knew, but his ghost is still supposed to be seen on very dark windy nights – but I've never seen anything and neither had my parents. A few years ago a neighbour just down the road told me that her son had seen the figure of a man running across this lower road, towards the mill. He reckoned he saw him as plain as day in his scooter headlights. So she asked me if I'd go with her one night, just along the road to see if we could see the ghost. Well, I met her at about 10.45 and we stuck it out until gone midnight, but didn't see a darned thing, apart from several owls hooting and flying low over our heads. None the less, I was quite glad to get back in the safety of my home. But what do you think of this?' she asked, as she handed me a piece of paper with the following story on it:

One autumn afternoon about the year 1831, just after the sun had sunk over the distant rim of the Cotswolds and the mists were stealing up from the Windrush, a large wagon containing the household goods of a family *migrating* from Witney to Worsham (a matter of 4 miles) in the valley, was rumbling along between Starvall Farm (now Whitehall) and Worsham Bottom. Sitting beside the driver were his wife and child.

Suddenly the two powerful horses became restive and seemed to see something ahead which inspired their terror. Then, up the rising road, a company of horsemen appeared. Although they were coming at a gallop, no sound was heard from the horses' feet. Their appearance did not arouse interest so much as cause apprehension – their laced coats, plumed hats and powdered wigs presented so unusual a sight as they swept up the hill, while their drawn swords gleamed in the faint afterglow from the sunset.

The driver jumped down and dragged his horses to the roadside as the cavalcade came on, but was astonished on finding it fading from his sight as it came alongside. His horses were lathering with fear, while the driver and his

wife could only glance at each other in terror. In another moment he was still more amazed, and called his wife to look round the tilt of the wagon, for the equestrian figures had again become visible and were galloping away towards Minster Lovell.

Minster Lovell, just along the road, is the next place that I shall visit on the Windrush. But now, with the winter sun setting and the mist rolling off the river, and tales of highwaymen and horsemen in powdered wigs and galloping horses running around in my head, I think it is time I got off home – and quick!

 ild March winds were sending clouds scurrying across a brilliant blue sky on the day when I dropped down the hill to Old Minster Lovell.

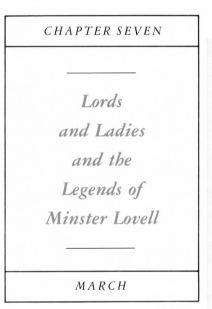

CHAPTER SEVEN

Lords and Ladies and the Legends of Minster Lovell

MARCH

I wandered over the stone bridge which spans the river Windrush, where bright yellow pussy-willows grew, looking like day-old chicks. In front of me stood the lovely Old Swan Inn, a gem of a place and a must for any traveller. The inn, which dates back to the fifteenth century, has great open fireplaces with inglenook seats on each side, and ancient blackened beams spanning the ceilings – and they serve up the most lovely food. Alongside the inn is a row of Cotswold stone built cottages, some roofed with local 'Stonesfield' slates, and some with warm yellow thatch. This same road leads to the lovely fifteenth century church of St Kenhelm, and to the ruins of Minster Lovell Manor House.

The Feast-day of the church is 17 July, and at one time free measures of home-made rhubarb wine, known locally as Rhubarb Jerkum, were served at the Old Swan to commemorate this day. The beautiful church was built around 1431 on the site of an earlier one. At the same time William, the seventh baron of Minster Lovell, built his manor house, also on the site of an earlier building.

As I walked down the lane leading to the ruins I was met with a chorus of jackdaws, dozens and dozens of them, jack-jacking away, until the air was filled

Delightful Old Swan Inn, Minster Lovell

with their cries. They were wheeling around and around the tall trees of the
ruined manor, some even looking as if they had started to build on the ledges of
the great walls, and from one of the trees came the unmistakable sound of a
woodpecker at work, searching for grubs in the bark. The chestnut trees had
already lost their treacly-brown protective covers and were displaying the palest
of green leaves.

There are several legends, part truth, part romance, and part hearsay,
haunting the ruins of Minster Lovell. The place has a kind of sadness and
ghostliness about it, so that it doesn't need a great imagination to believe some
of the stories.

When I was young I was friendly with a Mrs Pratley, whose forebears had
been Romanies, and who definitely had the gift of second sight. She used to go
to Minster Lovell and the surrounding villages in her old pony and trap, selling
clothes pegs, tapes and laces at the cottage doors. She was always telling me
stories about some of the strange things she saw on her rounds, especially at
Minster Lovell where the following story comes from.

'One autumn evening,' she told me, 'it was getting a bit dimpsy and the mist

Lords, ladies and legends at Minster Lovell Hall

was already lying low over the water meadows, shrouding the village and the manor ruins in a mysterious veil, when suddenly a figure of a white knight rose up in front of me. He was dressed in shining armour and he was astride a huge white charger. My pony shied, pulling the trap onto the side of the road. In a flash the rider and horse disappeared into the mist. I even saw the white breath coming from the animal's nostrils, and his long white tail was stretched out behind him.'

It was not until years afterwards that I heard the legend of Francis, ninth Lord Lovell, one of King Richard III's favourites. When the King was killed at the Battle of Bosworth, Francis Lovell knew that the King's enemies would seek him out and kill him, so he fled the battlefield. Later he took part in another battle at Stoke in 1487 fighting for Lambert Simnel, a man who claimed to be Richard, Earl of Warwick, and therefore lawful King of England. But King Henry VII's men were too good for them and Lord Lovell, noticing how the battle was going, left the battlefield. The story goes that he was last seen swimming his horse across the river Trent, but was unable to land owing to the steepness of the opposite bank; many people believed that he had drowned.

Others had a different theory: Lord Lovell, now a hunted fugitive, managed to get back to the great manor house at Minster Lovell, and with the help of a trusty manservant remained there, hidden in a secret room. The servant brought food and drink to his master daily, but locked him in the secret room every night. Years and years passed and the story was regarded as just another legend. But early in the eighteenth century some workmen were engaged in repairing the manor, and behind a great chimney-stack they made a startling discovery. Hidden in a small secret room they found the skeleton of a man seated at a table, with the skeleton of a small dog sitting at his feet. Folk believed that these were the remains of Francis, Lord Lovell – his trusty servant probably died suddenly, leaving his master entombed, to die of starvation.

Was the ghost of the white knight seen by Mrs Pratley that of Francis Lovell, trying to reach the

Celandines – heralds of spring

safety of his home? Whatever it was, Mrs Pratley told me that she saw the same ghost on several occasions along the same stretch of road, but not necessarily in the same place.

Another sad story of the ill-fated Lovells is told in the *Ballad of the Mistletoe Bough*.

The ballad is Victorian, but the sad death of Lord Lovell's bride took place many, many years earlier. It happened one Christmas time: one of the Lovells had been married that day, and there was lots of dancing and rejoicing. The beautiful young bride suggested a game of hide-and-seek – hoping her bridegroom would be the first to find her. She hid in one of the top rooms of the Manor in a big old oak chest – the lid closed fast, and became her grave.

Years later, it is said, the old chest was forced open, and there lay Lovell's beautiful bride. It was this tragic story which moved Thomas Haynes Bayley to write:

THE MISTLETOE BOUGH

The mistletoe hung in the castle hall,
The holly branch shone on the old oak wall;
And the Baron's retainers were blithe and gay,
And keeping their Christmas holiday.
The Baron beheld with a father's pride
His beautiful child – young Lovell's bride,
While she with her bright eyes seem'd to be
The star of the goodly company.
Oh! the mistletoe bough. – Oh! the mistletoe bough.
'I'm weary of dancing now,' she cried;
'Here tarry a moment, I'll hide; I'll hide
And Lovell, be sure thou'rt first to trace

The clue to my secret hiding place.'
Away she ran, and her friends began
Each tower to search and each nook to scan,
And young Lovell cried, 'Oh where dost thou hide!
I'm lonesome without thee, my own dear bride.'
Oh! the mistletoe bough. – Oh! the mistletoe bough.
They sought her that night and they sought her next day,
And they sought her again, when a week passed away;
In the highest, the lowest, the loneliest spot
Young Lovell sought wildly but found her not.
And years flew by, and their grief at last
Was told as a sorrowful tale long past;
And when Lovell appeared, the children cried,
'See, the old man weeps for his fairy bride.'
Oh! the mistletoe bough. – Oh! the mistletoe bough.
At length, an oak chest that long had laid hid
Was found in the castle; they raised the lid,
And a skeleton form lay mouldering there
In the bridal wreath of the lady fair.
Oh! sad was her fate! In sportive jest
She hid from her lover in the old oak chest;
It closed with a spring, and her bridal bloom
Lay withering there in a living tomb.
Oh! the mistletoe bough. – Oh! the mistletoe bough.

And that story is not just another legend, for the ancient oak chest is preserved at Grey's Court, Rotherfield Greys, near Henley in Oxfordshire, the mansion house of an estate which passed to William, seventh Lord Lovell, by his marriage in 1422 to Alice de Grey; the house now belongs to the National Trust and is open to the public.

At Ducklington, the village of my extreme youth, we had what we understood to be a piece of the Minster Lovell ruins. In the village meeting place that we called The Parish Room, which had once been a barn, there was a great wooden beam on which hung the coat-of-arms of the Lovells. At least, that was what the Reverend Tristram, the Rector of that time, told us it was; he said there were also some in the Rectory. In a book on Oxfordshire, I read that there was a fine old door somewhere in Ducklington which was known to have come from Minster Lovell old manor – but I have yet to trace it.

Walking up the cobbled driveway that leads to the part-ruined Great Hall, where the Lovells must have dined, one could easily let one's imagination run riot – could I really hear the faint music of the musicians in the gallery, and see the ghost-like figures of gallant knights and their fair ladies, wining, dining, and dancing . . . ?

Outside, and edging what had been the Great Courtyard, are the foundations of the other buildings, preserved so that parts of the manor, kitchens and other rooms can be traced. Near the riverside is what must have been one of the Lovell's fish-ponds, with the water reflecting the trees that surround it, and moorhens scooting about its banks. There were carpets of celandines under my feet; the milk or juice from the flowers was used at one time to get rid of warts. Clumps of green, shiny, red-splotched heart-shaped leaves of the cuckoo-pint, or 'Lords and Ladies' or wild arum, as it is probably better known, grew abundantly: in some areas it is called Jack-in-the-Hedge. This is a strange plant. From the heart-shaped, dark green leaves there comes a pale green sheath-like leaf; then inside this grows what is termed a spadix, which is part-male, part-female. After fertilisation, this will eventually be covered in bright red berries. The plant, by

the way, attractive as it looks, is poisonous. The fish-pond has had other uses over the years. One young man who was born and brought up in the village told me that the locals always called it 'The Doctors' Ditch'. This was because for many years several doctors relied on getting their leeches from there, which they used in their work. The young man also told me that his great-great-grandfather used to collect leeches for the doctors, and was himself treated with them during an illness he suffered in old age.

Lying just north of the ruins is the most wonderful dovecote that I have seen so far in my travels along the Windrush. It is perfectly rounded and like the manor is medieval. I peeped inside the tiny doorway. There are hundreds and hundreds of dove or pigeon nest-holes in there, with a cupola at the top for the birds to enter. The whole building is beautifully constructed, especially the roof, and is in a wonderful state of preservation. Nearby there are several great Cotswold barns and a lovely farmhouse, and the church, with the now quite wide river Windrush with its willow-bordered banks, sparkling in the sunshine and flowing silently on.

Back up the lane again, where several blackbirds were greedily eating the black shiny berries off the ivy-clad walls. Goosegrass

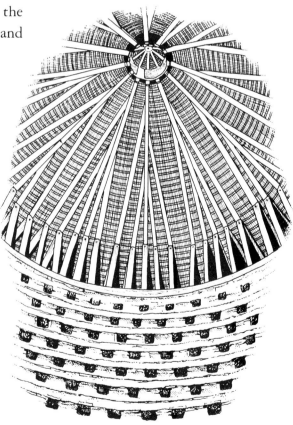

climbed up the hedge and red and white dead-nettles were blooming on the banks. At one time the white ones were eagerly sought-after by country folk to be used to make into tea, which was used as a home-made remedy for treating bronchitis. On the grass verge was a brilliant patch of violets, bluer than the spring sky above, and masses of primroses.

Opposite the Old Swan Inn there are wonderfully preserved buildings of what was once a mill, something to do with blanket-making – Witney is only three miles away – and the same young man who told me about the leeches also told me that a small field opposite the mill was always called 'The Racks', because at some stage in their making the blankets would have been hung up there to dry. Now the beautifully restored mill buildings are used as a conference centre.

The visitor must not get lovely Old Minster Lovell mixed up with New Minster Lovell, or Charterville Allotments, to give it its rightful name, which lies on the other side of the road and a bit further along the A4047.

Charterville Allotments was one of the settlements started by the Chartist leader Feargus O'Connor. In 1847 the National Land Company bought land here, and 78 single-storey dwellings were built, with good outbuildings and two or four acres, ready ploughed, to each dwelling. Instead of encouraging people who knew about tilling the land to live there, families from crowded northern towns were offered these places, by ballot. They were given £30 – and a pig – to start them off. But they didn't stay long, as they knew nothing about the trials and tribulations of running smallholdings. These unfortunate people had only been used to a back garden no bigger than a bed sheet, and were quite out of their depth. In no time at all they headed back to the crowded industrial north, and were never heard of again. Gradually, folk with more knowledge of growing things settled there; they specialised in plums, apples, tomatoes and flowers, and kept pigs and chickens; and some still do. Many of the country folk who made a go of it stayed on, with their children and grand-children taking over when the time came. Today, New Minster or Charterville Allotments is a splendid place to live – a far cry from the settlement that Feargus O'Connor started.

Hailey, Crawley, Curbridge and Cogges,
Witney Spinners and Ducklington Dogs.

I thought I would start with this local jingle because I shall be writing about Crawley, Cogges and Witney, but Ducklington Dogs will have to wait until the next chapter.

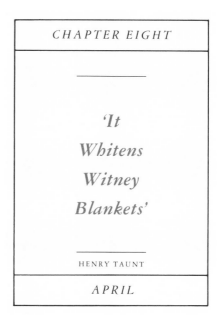

CHAPTER EIGHT

'It
Whitens
Witney
Blankets'

HENRY TAUNT

APRIL

It is said that in April spring takes two steps forward and one backwards, and that is certainly true of this year. On the day I had planned my next visit along the Windrush Valley the country woke up to a carpet of snow and it kept 'fithering' down all the morning. Yet two days previously we had had a perfect spring day, with hours of warm sunshine, and birds flashing through the air and several bees feeding on the spring flowers in my garden. But the biting cold winds that followed the snow were at least drying up the gardens and farmland, so at last some planting could be done. This is the sort of weather that my old grannie called 'Blackthorn winter' . . . 'We allus gets cold winds and frosts when the blackthorn's a-blooming,' she once told me. Her prediction was certainly running true to form this year, for the snow-white blossom was profuse in the hedgerows. This is the time of year when I earmark the best-looking blackthorn bushes, where, with a bit of luck, come October a goodly crop of sloes or slans (as they are often called) will be hanging blue and ripe, just right for making into sloe wine or distinctive sloe gin.

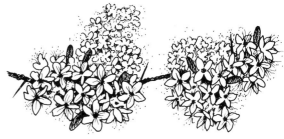

About ten days later, on a quiet cuckoo morning, when the soft south wind was blowing early butterflies into my garden and the countryside was wearing its beautiful new dress of gold, green and white, when the tide of spring was everywhere, and the soft ethereal green beeches were slowly unfolding their crumpled leaves, I set out for the village of Crawley, a couple of miles from Witney. Crawley still retains a bit of the Cotswolds with its grey stone cottages and inns, built on a hill overlooking the river Windrush, which is still winding, sparkling and flowing along.

All along the road the verges were banked with keck or cow parsley, while in the hedgerows the pink and white crab-apples blossomed. Overhead quite a number of plovers or peewits were rising and falling and gliding on the wind pockets in the sky above. Then suddenly some of them would dive at great speed, almost plummeting to the ground, only to glide upwards again: this is part of their spring courting display, and a joy to watch.

Of course, as in all the villages along the valley of the Windrush, there was a mill, which for years was used in some part in the manufacture of Witney blankets; now it is an industrial estate with several firms occupying different parts of the huge building, and the millhouse by its side has been beautifully restored.

Leaving the quiet, lovely village of Crawley, I took to the low-lying water meadows and walked by the riverside whose banks were gilded with knots of marsh marigolds, sometimes called kingcups or water bubbles. The fields were smothered with golden dandelions, reminding me to pick some soon for making into delicious home-made wine. And although these days we drink home-made wine for pleasure, in my gran's day all sorts of different wines were used for medicinal purposes; having the doctor cost money, so self-healing was much in evidence. Dandelion, for instance, was drunk as a tonic, to relieve indigestion and for a sluggish liver. You should always try to gather your dandelions on 23 April – St George's Day – providing the sun is shining.

Peewit sitting pretty

There was a pair of swans nesting on the river bank, one sitting tight on a nest of dried reeds while the other stayed near, guarding its mate. Several willow warblers warbled in the trees that skirted the river bank, and in a bush in the field I could hear the welcome sound of one of our summer visitors, the chiff-chaff; Billy Whitethroat is the country name for this bird, so easily recognised by its call 'chiff-chaff', repeated over and over again. In fact, the air was full of bird song. Somewhere near I could hear the fluting notes of a blackbird, skylarks sang high above in the sky and then, joy of joys! – about a dozen swallows, the first of the season, flew overhead. I began to think that I would never hear a cuckoo this spring. Friends had already heard them calling a couple of days before. Then, suddenly, there it was, the sound that we all look forward to hearing! He (I think it is the male that is first heard) was cuckooing away, trying to attract a female with his spring call. A clump of cowslips, one of the loveliest of our wild spring flowers, was growing at my feet. Gone are the days when we used to sit in fields absolutely smothered with them and make 'Tisty-Tosty' balls by bunching up about a dozen flowerheads and tying them with grass: this made a lovely soft sweet-smelling ball which we played a singing game with:

> 'Tisty-Tosty tell me true, who shall I be married to?
> Tisty-Tosty cowslip ball, at my sweetheart's name you'll fall'.

You went through the names of the village lads, hoping *not* to catch it at the boy you were sweet on! We also used to pick them for our mother to make into wine, but now the flowers are so scarce that they are a protected species.

Crawley mill

Chiff-chaffs come with spring to the Cotswolds

I wandered on and came to New Mill, which at one time was another offshoot of the manufacture of Witney blankets. Now the buildings are used by a 'high tech' development firm. Then, a bit further on, I came to what for many years was Witney's only bathing place; all the wooden huts where people changed were gone and so, too, was the diving board. All that was left were some stone steps leading into the river and the concrete built in to keep the bank-sides firm, and a path. This was where for years most of the older inhabitants of Witney had learned to swim. Now, of course, they can boast of a very up-to-date swimming pool in the centre of the town.

I had lingered too long at Crawley, and along the riverbank, so I put off my visit to Witney until another day. The next week I arranged to meet Richard Early, whose family have been making their world-famous Witney blankets for well over three hundred years. The huge new factory, blending with the old Witney mill, stands on the outskirts of the town. The firm of Charles Early is the longest-trading company in the United Kingdom; in 1960 one of the other blanket manufacturers in Witney, Marriotts, amalgamated with Early, but they still trade under the name of Charles Early (Witney) Limited.

In 1669 Thomas Early, then aged 14, was apprenticed to the blanket trade in Witney, and so began the Early dynasty. The manufacturing of the famous Witney blankets is now done all under one roof, but in the early days things were very different.

Back in the seventeenth century, with his apprenticeship over, young Thomas Early soon became a master weaver. It was the master weaver's job to buy and blend the wool and then send it out by pack-horse to the surrounding farms and cottages. Here the men would 'card' the wool while the women spun it into yarn and returned it to Witney, where it was hand-woven by the master weavers into what was called a 'stockful' – this was a long length weighing about

100 lb. At this point the 'blanket material' looked for all the world like sacking. Then this complete piece was sent off to the fulling mill and the next process was carried out there by the men called tuckers and fullers. This involved washing, shrinking and fulling, with the Windrush providing a generous flow of water. Fullers' Earth was a very vital commodity in the 'blanketing' process; it helped to clean the wool of oil and grease. Oil was added to the raw wool to improve its spinning qualities and, of course, the raw wool contained lanolin. So all this had to be washed out. The fulling of the cloth was part of a very important finishing process. The most primitive method of fulling was done by men beating the rough cloth with a heavy club in a vat of water, or laying the cloth in the Windrush, where the men would tread, stamp and walk about on the material. Much later human feet were replaced by two heavy wooden hammers, which were worked up and down by hand. These methods went out of date many years ago. Now, of course, the fulling is all done by modern machinery. Fullers' Earth is to be found below the layers of oolite stone in the Cotswolds. The 'stockful' was now shrunken and soft and the whole piece was 'tentered' or stretched on hooks (hence the word tenterhooks) outside on great wooden racks. After this the nap of the cloth was raised to make it fluffy; at one time this was done with prickly teazle-heads, fixed on a board. The teazles were grown especially for this job and can still be found all over the Cotswolds. Now, with the process complete, the 'stockful' was cut up into blankets.

Over the years the whiteness

Old Blanket Hall, Witney

and softness of Witney blankets have been attributed to the waters of the river Windrush by many people, and in 1667 Dr Robert Plot wrote: 'Some, I know, attribute a great part of the excellency of Witney blankets to the abrasive, nutritious water of the River Windrush, wherein they are scored.'

Gradually, over the years, machines for carding and spinning were introduced, but as late as 1837 the mills on the Windrush were still worked by water and not steam. There was no power-weaving until 1860.

Over the centuries many Witney blankets have been presented to royalty. In 1688 Thomas Early presented King James II with a pair of gold-fringed blankets. Then, in 1788, eighty-year-old John Early and Job Partlett, both at one time master weavers of the company, presented blankets to King George III and Queen Charlotte. Queen Mary received some when she visited Early's mill in 1941, and Queen Elizabeth II was also presented with some when she paid a visit in 1959.

World records in producing blankets and cloth have been created over the years: on 25 June 1811 a coat made at Newbury during one day only was worn on the evening of the same day by Sir John Throckmorton. The cloth had been produced in no more than eleven hours. [From Richard Early's book on Blanket Making.] On 8 June 1906, Early's sheared some sheep at sunrise and from it produced completed blankets by early afternoon, in the time of ten hours twenty-seven minutes. The company remained content with this record until 11 June 1969, three hundred years after Thomas Early was apprenticed. At 4 a.m. on that day, one hundred and fifty Kerry Hill sheep from a Cotswold farm were sheared on the mill premises. The wool passed through the various processes, and the first blanket was completed and enclosed in transparent wrapping by eleven minutes past noon. This new world record of eight hours eleven minutes is recorded in the *Guinness Book of Records*.

But that is not the whole of the story. Other blankets followed the first, until before evening fifty had been completed. One went to New York by Pan-Am airliner, and arrived in time to be displayed with a notice 'The wool of which this blanket is made was shorn from sheep at Witney, England, early this

morning'. It was a simple matter, of course, to see to the arrival of four other
blankets this same day, one in Paris, one in Milan, and two in London. A
sixth blanket was presented by Thomas Early's six-times-great-grandson to
William J. Vines, CMG, retiring Managing Director of the International
Wool Secretariat, for him to take to his newly-acquired sheep farm in
Australia.

Perhaps it is time for another record to be broken, as Charles Early (Witney)
Limited, with all the wonderful modern processes in their mill, move towards
the twenty-first century.

But blanket making is not the only thing Witney is famous for. During the
First World War, a lady called Ada Leonara Harris (no relation) used to visit her
old uncle and aunt who lived in West End, Witney. The town and the house and
her uncle and aunt so impressed her, that she wrote a song about it, which was
as popular with the Tommies as 'Pack up your Troubles':

IN AN OLD-FASHIONED TOWN

Words by Ada Leonara Harris

Music by W.H. Squire

There's an old-fashioned house in an old-fashioned street,
In a quaint little old-fashioned town,
There's a street where the cobble-stones harass the feet,
As it straggles up hill and then down;
And though to and fro' through the world I must go,
My heart while it beats in my breast,
Where e'er I may roam, to that old-fashioned home,
Will I fly back like a bird to its nest.

In that old-fashioned house in that old-fashioned street,
Dwell a dear little old-fashioned pair,
I can see their two faces, so tender and sweet,
And I love every wrinkle that's there.
I love ev'ry mouse in that old-fashioned house
In the street that runs up hill and down,
Each stone and each stick, ev'ry cobble and brick
In that quaint little old-fashioned town.

The river Windrush now passes behind the town, so I will join it later. In the meanwhile I'll take a wander down Witney High Street which still contains some nice old stone buildings, including the old Blanket Hall. But much has been altered over the past few years. The Market Square, which has recently been cleared of traffic, was where the cattle market was once held on each Thursday – 'Hurdle Thursday' as it was known locally, because of the hurdles that were put up on that day to keep in the cattle and sheep that were brought for sale. Just beyond the Market Square is the Town Hall, and the old Butter Cross, which was built in 1683 by William Blake of Cogges. It stands on thirteen stone pillars, and supposedly got its name from the habit of the local farmers' wives of congregating on the stone steps to sell their butter and other farm produce. On the top of the building there is a little tower which has a clock on two of its sides, on a third a sundial, and William Blake's name on the other. He also left money to be used for educational purposes in Cogges and in Witney. From there you can see the lovely spacious church green where once the Witney Feast was held each September. The green is dominated by the beautiful church of St Mary, with its tall slender spire. Look out for the little carved monkey about half way up: the story goes that many years

Old Butter Cross, Witney

ago, a man who was attending Witney Feast had a few animals on show. He had apparently been ill-treating them, including a little monkey. The frightened monkey managed to escape and in desperation ran up the spire of St Mary's church. It got about half-way up but could not go on, being ill-fed and young. It fell to its death, and the local people were so upset that they decided to remember the little monkey by placing a stone image of it on the spot on the spire where the animal had reached.

There is much to see inside the church, but look for the beautiful Wenman Chapel: the Wenmans were a powerful local family who were wool staple dealers in the Middle Ages. Nearby is the Grammar School, built in 1660 by Henry Box. Of course, over the years more up-to-date buildings have been added to the original ones; it is still one of the most important schools in the town. Close to the church are the marvellous excavations of the Bishop of Winchester's Palace which were carried out in 1984 by the Oxford Archaeological Unit. Queen Emma, wife first of Ethelred and then of Canute, and mother of Edward the Confessor, granted the bishops their Witney estate in 1044. Much of the building was done in the twelfth century. A booklet on the history of the Bishop's Palace is available locally.

Elegant church of St Mary's, Witney

But now I must make my way back to the river and to the hamlet of Cogges, where the Windrush divides into two separate rivers for the next five miles – just before it flows into the Thames.

Cogges is a delightful place, with its unique little church, so different from the other churches along the Windrush; its small tower is square at the base, octagonal above, and then has a conical roof that is set diagonally on it. Inside there is a lot to see, including the north chapel where there are carvings of animals playing musical instruments – there's a monkey playing a harp, and a goat with a pipe and tabor, and others, all of which I found most unusual. Then there is the lovely old vicarage, and a delightful manor house. The manor farm is now Cogges Farm Museum, which is open all spring and summer with demonstrations of country living – butter-making, farmhouse cooking, threshing and blacksmithing, sheep-shearing, and many other things. The farmhouse itself is open, with parts of it furnished in the style of the Edwardian period.

My problem now was to decide which arm of the river to follow; I thought the stream to the right, which leads to my beloved Ducklington, would be my best bet. Walking a little way along the river and ignoring the road and the super new stores and other shops that have grown up by its side, I came to what was in my young days a corn mill. Farm Mill is now empty, but I understand that soon it will be utilised for something more up to date. Across the meadows I picked out the tower of Ducklington village church.

Cogges church

Yellow-hammer

On a lusty May day, with the spring green still flooding the tree-tops, fields and hedgerows, I decided to make my way to Ducklington, which lies on the banks of the river Windrush about a mile from Witney. It was a warm, windy day with the shadows of the fast-moving clouds rushing over the lush fields. And although I am not truly *walking* all the way along the banks of the Windrush, today I thought that I would make my way to Ducklington along the gently

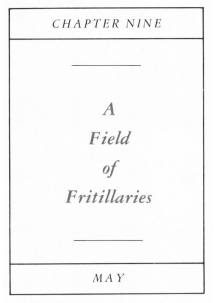

CHAPTER NINE

A
Field
of
Fritillaries

MAY

flowing right arm of the river, and listen to its soft music as it winds its way.

Before I set off I had a good look at the left arm, which today seemed rather rushing and deep, making the long green river weed move and sway like a maiden's tresses in the wind. We always called this left arm 'Tognall', and it was where at one time the 'gentlemen' of Witney supposedly bathed in the nude. All along Windrush-side blackcurrant, redcurrant and raspberry bushes grow in the centre of the old willow trees, where the birds have left seeds – as youngsters we greedily ate them. Just at this point, but on the left arm of the Windrush, there are oaks, ash and silver birch trees growing out of the willows which are now much higher than the willow branches. I wonder whether someone planted these purposely? – for I've never seen anything like it before.

The rivers at this point are only a field apart, but soon the left arm begins to meander over the field eastwards, although there's never more than a couple of miles between them. Gone now are the Cotswold hills with their windswept uplands and deep valleys which give the area much of its characteristic beauty. From now on my journey will be made through the lovely flat low-lying meadows of the Windrush valley. So, taking the right-hand side of the river, I started to walk towards Ducklington.

The river was teeming with wildlife, and coots, moorhens and mallard ducks, all with babies, quickly scooted their families away as I approached. I spotted several fish, too – carp, I think they were. Yellow flags bloomed on the river's edge, and sweet, heavy-smelling May blossom foamed and fell from the hawthorn bushes. Away over to the left, field after field of brilliant yellow oil-seed rape glowed in the sunshine. Such a lot of farmers seem to be going in for this crop now.

It was in the Windrush, and very near to where I was standing, that my brothers and cousins used to go crayfishing on summer nights, for in those days the river was teeming with them and they made us a very good meal now and then.

The night had to be dark, not moonlight, or a shadow cast on the water would send the little crab-like creatures scurrying away. But we country folk – not accustomed to electric light either in our homes or in the streets – were used to finding our way about on dark nights, and could actually see quite well. You needed a bit of rancid meat or a smelly dead bird to catch your crayfish. You placed the meat into a home-made wire cage, then this was gently lowered into the water; hopefully the crayfish would go into it, attracted by the smell. Here the catcher had to concentrate all the while, gazing into the river-bed. Then, a slight tug on the string that operated the little wire door and, hey presto! you probably caught half a

Fritillary field on a cuckoo morning

dozen of the little beggars. The pattern was repeated over and over again, until you had caught a bucketful. Of course, they had to be kept alive until they were tipped into a saucepan of boiling water and cooked. Once, when my cousin Harry was a lad, he went off crayfishing and brought home a bucketful, setting it down on the living room floor of their cottage. It was a bit late so the family went off to bed with a promise to cook the crayfish first thing in the morning. In the morning, loud screams from his mother brought everyone running downstairs. Overnight the crayfish had climbed out of the bucket and had gone awandering, and they were everywhere – even in the ashes in the fire-grate.

Then I reached the spot in the river that we always called 'Gooseham', where all summer long most people went bathing. During the school holidays we practically lived there. It was here that I taught myself to swim; several others were doing the same, with the more experienced swimmers rushing and diving and splashing about. We youngsters copied the older ones with arm and leg movements: I can still taste that river water as time and time again I went under, only to emerge coughing and spluttering, until I mastered the art of swimming. And in those days several of the fields near to the village were where the wild fritillaries grew. As soon as we knew that they were showing bud, always when the kingcups are in flower, we would rush down there, grabbing and snatching at the purply-pink spotted 'snakes' heads', as we called them, for that is what they resemble when they are in bud, although some folks say that they look like plovers' eggs. And what a thrill if we happened to find a white fritillary – they were very rare. Mind you, we had to be quick off the mark, otherwise if a band of gypsies knew that they were out, they would pick every flower, and go on the train to Oxford and sell them. But now things have changed.

A very wise man, a Mr Peel who lived with his wife at the manor house in Ducklington, realising the rarity of the fritillaries, in 1963 bought a field where they grew, to save the flowers from extinction. Because of his foresight, the field will forever grow the wild fritillaries. And whereas when we were children just a few flowers grew there, now each May it is massed with them, because no one is allowed to pick them; and the folk at Ducklington hold a 'Fritillary Sunday' each May, so that people can come from far and wide to enjoy these lovely, rare flowers. The farmer who rents the field has to vacate it by March and is not

Barn owl, all too rare a sight

allowed to go and cut the grass for hay until the first of July.

I turned left from the river to go into the fritillary field, which was still massed with them in the third week in May, along with lots of cuckoo flowers (Lady's Smock), cowslips, buttercups, daisies and sorrel – we used to eat the bitter leaves of this plant – and here and there I found a few quaking-grass. Moon daisies and ragged robins were in bud, and by the ditch-side late marsh marigolds were still blooming, and the lush green hedge was full of yellow-hammers. Cuckoos were calling on this perfect early summer day, and several magpies were busily searching the hedgerows; they are handsome birds and I am quite fond of them, but they do rob the nests of other birds, taking eggs and fledglings. Of course I am very superstitious about magpies, and bow my head and say 'good morning, sir' to all I see – bad luck if you don't! This I do wherever I am, and get some very funny looks sometimes!

I wandered up the lane towards the village, over the bridge that spans the Windrush, and passed what used to be Farmer Druce's great stone barns, where we used to sneak in and pinch locust-beans – really meant for cattle feed. Now, the beautiful barns have been made into elegant homes. Nearby there was a willow-bed, known locally as Buffy's Raddam, where the old village basket-maker grew his willows. I came to the church of St Bartholomew, which dates from the eleventh century and is built in the Transitional Norman, Early English and Perpendicular styles. The altar cloth is wonderful, and very unusual: it was made and embroidered by Mrs Peel, wife of the man who bought the fritillary field, and depicts several of the lovely mauve fritillaries. Near the church is the old village school, which I attended until I left at the age of fourteen; it is still used, along with a modern building. Opposite the old school is the village pond, which fairly recently has been cleaned out and landscaped and now the three features – church, school and pond – make a lovely group.

During the last war the village was plagued with flies – millions of them settled inside and outside the houses. The trouble started because the local refuse dump, where stuff from miles and miles away was dumped, was not allowed, because of the blackout, to light the fires which normally burnt much of the rubbish and therefore the flies and their eggs. People were at their wits'

Ducklington church and pond

end, fly papers and fly spray were bought, but nothing stopped the onsurge of flies. The Parish Council was approached, and duly reported to the Witney Rural Council, who promptly sent a man to find out more about the trouble. The man – not a local – was talking to one of the Ducklington men about the problem and asked, 'What sort of flies are they?' 'Ah, they be they blue-assed 'uns,' came the reply. The newcomer, realising that the village of Aston was three or four miles away, said, 'You don't mean to tell me that they fly over from Aston to here?' – not knowing that 'blue-assed flies' are a local name for a type of blow-fly.

Near the church is the lovely big old rambling rectory, though the rector now lives in a modern house further up in the village. The present owners, Mr and Mrs Craig, have made it into a wonderful home, keeping the structure much as it was. In the kitchen there is a delightful old larder door with several holes bored in it to let air through, and inside are carved the initials and date of the man who made and fixed it – T.S. September 5th, 1726. I was taken right up to the top of the house to the roof space, or attics. Here there were four or five huge oak beams which made up part of the roof structure. They have coats-of-arms and fleur-de-lys painted on them, and are believed to have come from the great Manor House at Minster Lovell. Here is a letter to the owner from John Steane, Keeper of the Field Section of the Oxford Museum Services:

I have recently had a letter from Michael Maclagan, Portcullis Herald, who tells me that there is not much doubt about the two Coats of Arms which are painted on your beams. The first one is for Deincourt and the heraldic description is Argent fess dancetty between ten billets sable. This he thinks occurs on the fine tomb in Minster Lovell Church. The second is for Poynings and the heraldic description is Barry of six or and vert a bend gules. He thinks that the badge looks as though it might be a fetter lock and indeed, a square cornered padlock was the badge of Francis Viscount Lovell. Mr Maclagan's recollection is that there certainly was a Lovell-Deincourt marriage but he cannot, at the moment, recall an alliance with the Poynings family. The

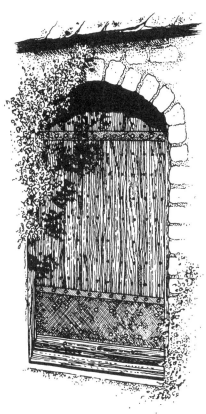

white fleurs-de-lys on a blue ground might well refer to the arms of Holland from whom the Lovells derived a barony (Azur, semé of lys and a lion rampant argent). He imagines that the yellow or gold lions and the fleurs-de-lys represent the royal arms and a token of loyalty.

Having found the beams I was keen to find out about the old oak door that is also said to have come from Minster Lovell about the same time. I made several enquiries but could find out nothing for certain. A few days later the telephone rang. It was Mrs Ann Coles who lives in a nearby village. She had heard of my interest and said that she could fill in most of the details about the door, as it had been in their cottage at Ducklington for years. 'We lived in that cottage opposite the old baker's; the door, which we painted white, never fitted very well and let in the draught something terrible. So, as soon as we bought the cottage, we took it out and put it in an old shed where we kept the hens' food and things. A lady called Mrs Williams, who was living at Rectory Cottage, Yelford, heard about the door and offered to buy it. She had it fitted up as her front door, and as far as I know it is still there.'

After a telephone call or two I visited Rectory Cottage, now the home of Dr Clegg, and lo and behold, there it was! a very, very old door, believed to be fifteenth-century, covered with huge blacksmith-made iron studs. From what I have been able to piece together, it seems fair to say that the door *is* the one from Minster Lovell. Whether it was once used in Ducklington Old Manor, we don't know (no one seems to know exactly where that was), but that is something the local History Group hope to find out.

Back in Ducklington I went down the road towards what was once Holtom's Roller Flour Mills, which for many years used the Windrush to drive its huge water-wheel. I remember having many a ride home from Witney on one of Holtom's flour carts. Carter Porter used to sit up front covered in a fine white dust of flour, even his eyelashes were powdered with it. Sometimes he would have three or even four great cart-horses in the shafts, depending on the load. In summertime the horses wore little caps over their ears to keep the flies from worrying them. When Carter Porter took a load of flour to Witney station to be put on to the train, he would fling great big nosebags around the horses' necks while the waggon was being unloaded, and they would stand and munch away contentedly. When their bags were nearly empty they would toss them up, flinging their heads high to enable them to get all the bits at the bottom of the nosebag.

Just outside the main mill building there was a thatched granary store built on staddle stones, to keep the rats out; but now the granary has gone and the old mill house, and so, too, have the carters and their horses – *and* the flour. In 1972 the river Windrush itself was directed away from the mill in a wide sweep. This happened after the mill was sold to a firm called Oldacres, who dealt in animal feeds; the buildings are now much bigger than originally, and the last I heard the mill had been sold again, to Unigate.

One reminder of the past from Holtom's Flour mill is a white paper bag, which would have held 3 lb of flour; it was given to me by one of the old mill workers, and has the words printed on it:

'WINDRUSH PRIDE'
SELF-RAISING FLOUR
MILLED and PACKED by
HOLTOM and SONS LTD.
Ducklington Mills
Witney, Oxon.

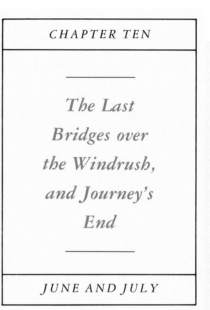

I n the meadows just below Ducklington Mill I started the last part of my journey along the Windrush. It was early June.

Still the river wound its way in great loops, and still the drunken willow trees bordered it. The many willow trees along the greater part of the Windrush began as mere posts, which in the early years would have had barbed wire attached to them, to keep the cattle from the steep banks – and, then, like Topsy, they just grew and grew. Quite often some of them are pollarded, but others have just been left to grow long branches which give shade to the cattle and provide roosting places for many birds. I reached the area known locally as The Ford, which is in the middle of a great plantation. Here a wooden foot-bridge spans the river and there still is a ford there, which is the entrance to some of the meadows. By the side of the ford is what must be the biggest, most glorious chestnut tree anywhere, and today it is at its best, displaying thousands and thousands of creamy flowers. 'Whitsuntide candles' is the country name for them, for that is what the blossom of the conker-tree looks like – giant candles set in great green candle-sticks. This is a view many locals will want to cherish, because in a few years' time the countryside around here will have been changed dramatically. Unfortunately for the folk living in this area, but not for the businessmen, this part of Oxfordshire lies on a huge bed of gravel. Already hundreds of acres near here have suffered from gravel extraction,

The Ford, on the way to Hardwick

at nearby Hardwick, Stanton Harcourt and Standlake. And now it is Ducklington's turn, although at this point it is about a mile from the village.

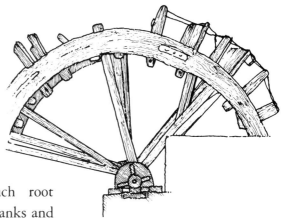

But my thoughts today must concentrate on the glorious summer scene. There are lots of huge beech trees here with much root exposed, clutching the sides of the banks and looking for all the world like giant grey fingers. The sun shone through the leaves, dappling the water, until it looked as if the very stream was dancing. In the shade of the tree-filled plantation I noticed something blue under a bush. Walking towards it I saw a patch of late bluebells, so very, very blue, looking as if a piece of the summer sky had fallen there. Millions of insects flew and danced over the water, dragonflies with transparent wings ('fairy bombers' was my very young son's wartime name for them) floated on the gentle breeze, and over in the meadows cattle grazed, swishing their tails like pendulums to keep the flies at bay.

At the end of the plantation I came to the Fish House with its castle-like tower and nice stone-built house attached to it. I talked to Mrs Hudson who has lived there for several years. She told me that originally it had been a fulling mill, then later became a corn mill. Around 1707 Cokethorpe House was built about half a mile away and about 1725 the owners made the castle-like building into a folly, adding the finials and gargoyles which give it its ancient appearance. Then it became a pump-house, to pump water from the Windrush up to Cokethorpe House, still using the old wooden water-wheel that had previously driven the mill. The wheel, which is still there, is a very old example of wooden wheel-making, with compass arms. This method of pumping water to the 'big house' went on until 1950, when electricity was installed in the Fish House and cottage and in Cokethorpe House. Ten years later, all the houses in that area were connected with Witney (Worsham) water. Since then the old mill wheel has been silent. I was told that the name 'Fish House' came about because earlier occupiers of the house had to supply Cokethorpe House regularly with fish caught in the mill pool.

The Fish House, on the bank of the Windrush below Ducklington

Today there are still plenty of fish in the mill pool, which is bordered with yellow flag flowers. On the bankside thistles vie with pollen-laden grasses and giant foxgloves, and the meadow beyond is filled with summer flowers – red clover, purple vetch, agrimony, bright yellow buttercups and lush green grass, just waiting to be cut and made into sweet-smelling hay.

A little further along the river I came to the pretty little hamlet of Hardwick where the mill there has been made into attractive workshops. The owner, Pat Hamilton, who also lives in the lovely mill-house with her family, is a very skilled silversmith; she has a workshop there along with two potters. The old mill wheel has gone but there is quite a lot of the mill 'furniture' left – wooden corn storage bins and a wonderful 'flour selector', along with wheels and cogs that helped to drive the little mill, which was still grinding meal for animal feed up until the outbreak of the Second World War. The granary and cart sheds are still there and all the mill buildings are very well preserved, with a lovely carved stone door surround that was rescued from the nearby ruins of Eynsham Abbey: also from the Abbey is a unique tombstone, used as part of the floor in the wheel chamber. The piece that is visible shows the carved head of an abbot, complete with mitre. In the mill house there is a huge stone over the fireplace, and historians have told the owners that that, too, came from the Eynsham Abbey ruins.

Several swallows who had nests in the mill buildings were flying low over the water, and every now and then there was a plop as a fish, probably a brown trout, rose to catch its supper. There were hens scratching about in the yard, one with ten chicks that had hatched out the day before. A horse poked its sleek head from its stables and a mother cat lay on the flagstones outside the kitchen door while her five kittens played and rolled over her. An idyllic summer scene on that lovely June evening.

A few days later I resumed my journey. I left the hamlet of Hardwick, walked up the road, passing great Dutch barns belonging to the farm nearby, and on to a bridge where the road crosses over the Windrush. Since leaving Cogges I have been travelling on the right arm of the river, but just half a mile along this road the left arm passes under the road at Beard Mill. I thought that as I was so near I would like to pay it a visit, remembering from my young days that we used to cycle along there on our way to visit Stanton Harcourt. But the thing that has

Mole and mushrooms

always stuck in my mind about Beard Mill was what I always thought were the skeletons of lots of rats and mice nailed up on the wooden sides of the old cart shed: mind you, I never looked too closely, but Harry Trinder who was born in the mill house and lived there for many years told me that they were in fact mole skins that had been stretched and nailed up there to dry. These would most likely have fetched sixpence each in those days. He also told me that the mill – a three-storey building – had stopped grinding barley for cattle feed around the 1920s. I asked him the reason for this, and he said that it was a job to keep enough water back to run the mill because the sluice gates which helped to build up the water pressure were in a bad state and the owner wouldn't have them repaired. There is a stone set into the wall of the old privy, the contents of which at one time went straight into the Windrush: on the stone is carved a date – 1575 – but there was most likely a mill there before then. You can still see the marks on the side walls of the wheel chamber, made by the two huge mill wheels, twelve feet in diameter and four feet wide, as they splashed round and round.

Beard Mill, Hardwick

Now this mill, too, has been made into workshops for artists and craftsmen, all working in different mediums: painting, silk printing, sculpture and picture framing. But I must retrace my steps to the right arm of the Windrush, and then it is only a few miles before the two arms converge.

Now the countryside looks quite different – miles and miles of golden gravel pits, with huge machines for extracting the gravel towering above the trees, and a constant flow of lorries being loaded. Some of the pits have been left as nature reserves with coot and moorhen, great and little crested grebes, herons and martins finding homes there too. Other pits have been filled in and reverted to farmland, while some provide facilities for water-skiing and picnic areas, with the river Windrush still winding and flowing along nearby. Then I went on to what had once been Underdown Mill, and then to Church Mill at Standlake, just in sight of St Giles's church with its octagonal tower topped with a slender spire.

There has been a mill on this site for nine hundred years. Its first job was that of a fulling mill and its last, during the Second World War, was to grind both flour and cattle feed. Then for forty years the mill wheel was silent. Now the mill has been beautifully restored. The restoration was done over five years ago

Restored Church Mill at Standlake

Standlake church and cow parsley

by the then owner Peter Ross, and in 1983 when every part had been overhauled the mill was declared viable once more. It is in a most delightful setting, with peacocks and grey wagtails strutting about on the lawns. The mill pool, along with its own stretch of the Windrush, is filled with fish of every kind. Garlands of dog roses and honeysuckle climb and fall over the bushes in the mill's meadow, and the sharp, tangy smell of the elder-flowers in the hedge remind me to make wine and champagne with the creamy blossoms.

I left this lovely scene, and walked down towards the church and village. Unfortunately the church was locked so I continued down the village street, where the Windrush runs beside the roadside cottages for a little way. I was about a quarter of a mile out of the village when I heard the familiar sound of rushing water (all mills have a mill-race or weir) as it pounded over the weir at Gaunt House Mill. Unfortunately the owner was unavailable, but the peaceful setting and delightful gardens, full of July bird-song, made it a very desirable place.

Back on the road I came to Broad Bridges, where the road crosses over both arms of the river Windrush, which are now only seventy yards apart.

Nearby is Gaunt House, which happens to be on the left arm of the river. Gaunt House is a beautiful, moated manor house, said to have been first built in the fifteenth century by John Gaunt. It suffered a very severe siege in 1643 when King Charles's troops held it. Cannon-balls were later found in the garden and also in the deep moat which is fed from the Windrush. More cannon-balls resulted from another fierce battle between the Roundheads and the King which took place on 29 May 1645, and yet another attack was made on 1 June of that year. The house was rebuilt sometime after this. Today it is a peaceful place, still with some of its ancient grandeur, its lovely moat a setting for the beautiful old house.

I made my way back to the roadway and Broad Bridges, then climbed through a fence to see just where the two arms converge. Now the Windrush had become a broad, reed-filled river in the very last mile of its thirty-mile journey. But it still had one more mill on its bank – and so I came to Newbridge Mill, the last of the Windrush mills. All that is left is a pleasant house and garden and a great wide rushing weir, foaming, frothing and cascading to sweep under the road and flow under the very last of the Windrush bridges.

Soon after it left the last mill, the river seemed to take on a quieter, calmer look, as if it were savouring the last few hundred yards. But there was still plenty of wildlife on its bank. A tree creeper just the colour of the bark ran quickly up the trunk of a tree, and from a hawthorn bush a spotted fly-catcher made a sudden darting flight to catch an insect before returning to its perch, repeating the same pattern over and over again. A reed bunting with its hooping flight flew from bush to reed and back again several times – it probably had a nest of youngsters near and was nervous of my presence. That little meadow – where my story ends – was filled with masses of wild flowers and grasses, moon daisies, ragged robins and hens-and-chickens, and on the riverside pink mallow and blue meadow cranesbill.

Every bush had dog roses clambering over it, their petals like confetti spilled on to the grass. A solitary foxglove (sometimes called 'witches' bells') stood on guard by the waterside, several big, brown velvet bumble bees disappearing into its bell-like flowers.

Now the end was very near. I had travelled throughout the year, in foul weather and fine. I had come out of the Cotswold hills on to the broad flat flower-filled meadows of Oxfordshire. Slowly and quietly, my beloved Windrush slipped unobtrusively into Mother Thames, to disappear under the great arches of New Bridge.

I had reached the end of my journey.

Journey's end

Cider Making

During a visit to Naunton one summer Mr Bert Davis told how he used to help with the cider making as a boy.

The trough was first swilled with water from the Windrush brook and the horse was harnessed. As the cider-mill at Naunton was the only one in the district, farmers from a wide area brough their apples here to be crushed by the stone wheel. This method crushed the pips as well, and it was the crushed pips that gave the cider much of its flavour. Drawing the heavy stone wheel round and round in the trough was very hard work and the horses were changed frequently. The farmers would often use their own horses and while they were resting they were stabled in what is now the mill-end of cottage No.5 The Quadrangle. As the cider-mill belonged to the owner of the bake-house a local man was always in charge of the proceedings, but helpers would be hired, or farmers would bring their own men.

The apples were always tipped into the trough behind the wheel so that the horse could 'start easy'. After crushing, the pulp was placed in a wooden press, layers of pulp alternating with coconut matting. Oak boards were placed on top and screwed down. This was very hard work and needed all the strength the men could muster. The resulting pulp was now in the form of cakes as hard as bricks. These cakes were loaded onto the carts, together with the barrels of juice, and were used to feed pigs, or as fuel. The coconut matting was then washed in the brook Windrush, and hung up to dry. On reaching home the juice was transferred to hogsheads, there to mature for three to four years. Those who could manage it liked to travel to Birmingham for their large barrels or hogsheads and try to buy those that had been used to import rum. Once a barrel had been used for cider it could never be used for anything else, because the new cider was very acidic and would eat into the wood, giving the taste of cider to anything else that might be put into it. To counteract this biting acidity wheat was added. Some farmers added meat, or a young piglet. Everything that was

---

added disappeared completely, the resulting cider after maturing being crystal clear. It was never drunk out of glasses, which were said to spoil the flavour, but out of earthenware mugs or horns. Mr Davis has one of these horns at home.

During harvesting and threshing each man took his own horn and food with him for the day, and the farmer would make regular calls for 'tots'. Each man's horn was filled by the 'totter-out' whose principal job this was. The cider was carried to the fields each day. 'My, how it made us work,' said Mr Davis. 'I don't think you'd get much work out of anyone with today's chemical stuff.' As far as Mr Davis could remember the crushing of the apples cost the farmer about a shilling.

These notes were given to me by Mrs E. Garner of Naunton

Mallard on the Windrush

The Windrush River

Thro' the Cotswolds night and day,
Thro' the valley 'neath the hill,
Windrush wend your winding way,
Sometimes rushing, sometimes still.
Down the seasons you will travel,
Singing out your songs of praise,
Raging thro' those Cotswold winters,
Babbling thro' the summer days.
On your everlasting journey,
Past the lichen covered mill,
Thro' the village, past the churchyard
Nestling snugly on the hill.
Children play within your reaches,
Old folk pass the time of day,
You can see them, you can hear them,
As you wend along your way.
River Windrush you must hurry,
You are nearing journey's end,
Say goodbye to those green Cotswolds,
Soon you'll join old Father Thames.

J.E. Sharpe

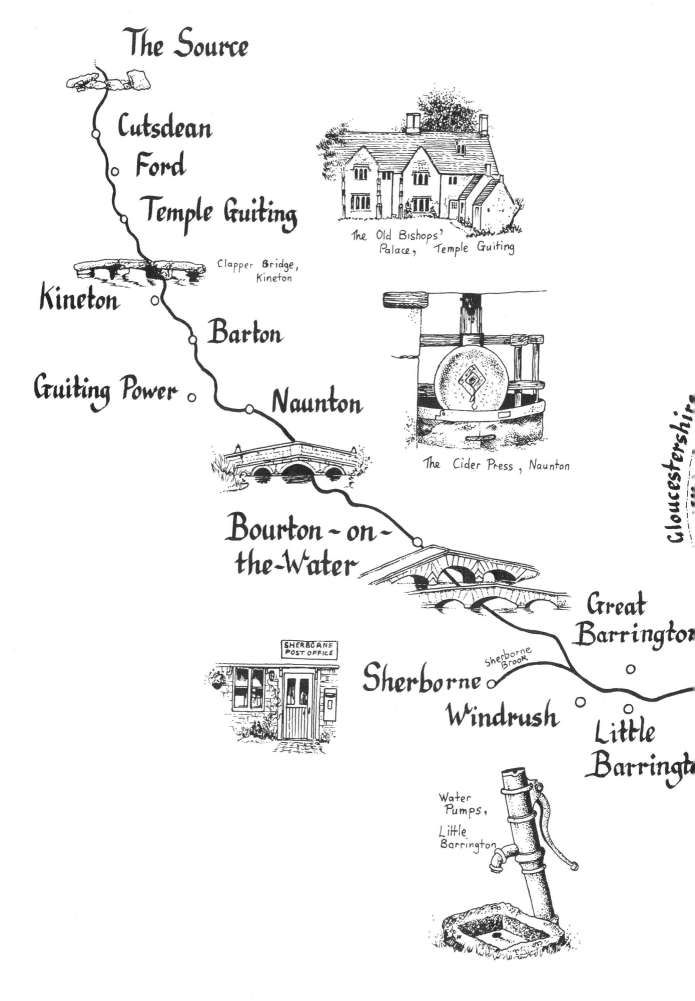

The Source

Cutsdean

Ford

Temple Guiting

The Old Bishops'
Palace, Temple Guiting

Clapper Bridge,
Kineton

Kineton

Barton

Guiting Power

Naunton

The Cider Press, Naunton

Bourton - on -
the-Water

Great
Barrington

SHERBORNE
POST OFFICE

Sherborne

Sherborne
Brook

Windrush

Little
Barrington

Gloucestershire

Water
Pumps,
Little
Barrington